Do the dead speak to us? Do they offer guidance? Do our deceased loved ones drop by for visits? What about poltergeists? Do angels have wings? What about mythical monsters? Is there a difference between a ghost and a spirit?

Mediums are touted for their abilities to communicate with the dead, but can anyone make contact? Where do aliens fit in to the picture, and are they somehow related to the dead? What about alien abductions? Do they really happen?

These are all questions we'll consider as we attempt to explain the unexplainable!

Panta Rei Press is an imprint of Crossroad Press Publishing

Copyright © 2015 by Rob MacGregor
Cover illustration by Dave Dodd
Design by Aaron Rosenberg
ISBN 978-1-941408-57-5
For information address Crossroad Press at 141 Brayden Dr., Hertford, NC 27944
www.crossroadpress.com

First edition

BUMP
IN THE
NIGHT

GHOSTS, SPIRITS AND ALIEN ENCOUNTERS

ROB MacGREGOR

PANTA REI

INTRODUCTION

THE SPIRIT OF HALLOWEEN

Halloween: it's known as the day when the veil between worlds of the living and the dead is the thinnest.

In pagan times, it was the eve of Samhain—pronounced sow'-en or sow'-ween—the end of the Celtic year, the beginning of winter, and the day when the dead were said to rise from the grave and walk the earth. Like many pagan holidays, it was Christianized in the Middle Ages as a Catholic vigil observed on the eve of All Saints Day, November 1—All Hallows Eve. Regardless of its origin, it was a day when homages for the dead were observed, and eventually it became linked with spooks, ghosts, all things that go bump in the night.

While Halloween is the day of reckoning for such matters, tales of ghosts, haunted houses, and phantom ships are timeless matters. Questions about life after death is a perennial interest as is contact with the other side. It's an unsolved mystery—maybe the most important mystery of all. While mainstream science says there is no proof that the dead survive or can be contacted, others are convinced by their own personal experiences.

Do the dead speak to us? Do they offer guidance? Do our deceased loved ones drop by for visits? What about poltergeists? Do angels have wings? Mediums are touted for their abilities to communicate with the dead, but can anyone make contact? Where do aliens fit into the picture, and are they somehow related to the dead? What about alien abductions? Do they really happen?

These are all questions that we'll consider. But let's start with basics. What's the difference between a ghost and a spirit? Generally speaking, a ghost haunts, a spirit guides.

A ghost might be considered an energy form that performs repetitive actions related to the life of a person who spent considerable time in the place where the haunting is occurring. In that sense, they are energy shells lacking conscious awareness. Ghosts are also sometimes described as spirits that are stuck between the physical world and the afterworld. They might be clinging to physical existence and not even aware they are dead. In that sense, they are unintentional intruders, and might even believe they are still alive, that the people living in their houses are the annoying ghosts.

A spirit, on the other hand, is usually defined as the non-physical aspect of a deceased person who has moved into the afterlife and might come back to guide or comfort. Deceased family members and friends are the most likely spirits to come for a visit.

Usually, when such contact is made, it's initiated by the living. The ancient Greeks journeyed to the Oracle of the Dead to contact the deceased. In the 16th century, John Dee used an Aztec mirror to make contact. In the mid-19th century, the Fox Sisters ignited the Victorian awakening to the spirit world with their peculiar communications with 'Mr. Splitfoot.' In the late 20th century, author Raymond Moody, inspired by the ancient Greeks, created a 'psychomanteum,' a chamber to contact the dead.

Today, the Cassadaga Spiritualist Camp in Central Florida and the Lily Dale Spiritualist Assembly in Lily Dale, New York remain havens for mediums who give voice to the dead. But do mediums really contact the dead? It's a matter of opinion. Some mediums are uncanny in their abilities to read and advise their clients. Others might be frauds, plying age-old tricks to impress. But there are also other possible means to make contact, such as dreams, radio signals, photography, and Ouija boards.

But are ghosts and spirits real?

Mainstream scientists often attribute ghostly experiences to environmental factors or illusions produced by the brain. In fact, in some cases, there are logical explanations for mysterious phenomena. But when more than one person witnesses a ghost, such explanations fall short.

"To be open-minded and not sure is a good thing; it just means the person has not had enough of a ghostly encounter to move beyond skepticism," writes Louis Charles author of Helping Ghosts.

"Yet, they remain open to the possibility. To the cynic, however, their mind is made up and closed. They will not believe in ghosts even if they become one themselves...perhaps."

Interestingly, open-mindedness is sometimes limited to a particular phenomenon. Many who are willing to believe in ghosts dismiss UFOs as something from the realm of science fiction and fantasy. The same goes for hard-core UFO/alien believers. Ghosts are snubbed. In fact, purveyors of the ancient alien scenario might tell you that legends of ghosts and spirits were actually stories about aliens in disguise. The two phenomena typically don't mix well.

However, in terms of what goes 'bump in the night,' we can't ignore the alien abduction phenomena. And, what's really weird is that possibly the two phenomena—ghosts/spirits and aliens/ UFOs—are somehow related. We'll take a deeper look at that matter later in the book.

ASIDE:

A third of Americans say they believe in ghosts, according to an AP-Ipsos poll conducted in 2007. While 34 percent are believers, 23 percent claim they have encountered a ghost or believe they have been in one's presence. Three in ten have awakened sensing a strange presence in the room. People most likely to see a ghost are singles, Catholics, and those who never attend religious services.

Skeptical Inquirer surprisingly found out in a 2006 survey that the more educated you are, the more likely you are to believe in ghosts and other paranormal phenomena. Contrary to expectations, a poll of 439 college students found seniors and grad students were more likely than freshmen to believe in haunted houses, psychics, telepathy, channeling and other mysterious phenomena.

While 23 percent of college freshmen expressed a general belief in paranormal concepts—from astrology to communicating with the dead—31 percent of seniors did so and the figure jumped to 34 percent among graduate students.

So it's a smart idea to keep your mind open to the possibility that ghosts and spirits not only exist, but can communicate with us.

As for aliens, nearly half of Americans believe they are driving those UFOs that so many have seen. In a 2002 Sci Fi Channel-Roper Poll, 48% say they believe that UFOs, piloted by alien beings, have visited the earth in some form over the years. More than a third of Americans (37%) believe that humans have already interacted with extraterrestrial life forms. Of those, 57% believe the alien abduction phenomenon is real, but only 10% of the general population believe in alien abductions. That's probably because the idea is just too spooky!

PART ONE
HAUNTINGS

1

HAUNTED PLACES

Ghosts, it seems, prefer the indoors. That's where most are seen, and they're usually linked to a house or building. The exception might be that home away from home—the graveyard. But what self-respecting ghost would prefer a cemetery—even a mausoleum—over the ritzy digs of say the famed Dakota?

THE DAKOTA BUILDING

Situated at Central Park West and 72nd Street, the majestic structure housing 64 co-op apartments stands across from New York City's Central Park. It's high gables, terracotta features, and gargoyles give the Victorian era building an imposing presence, a hint of its opulence and mystery.

While the Dakota once housed some of the world's most famous people, such as Judy Garland, Leonard Bernstein and Lauren Bacall, the building is best known for being John Lennon's last home and the site of his tragic murder on Dec. 8, 1980. Lennon's ghost supposedly haunts the Dakota, according to several witnesses. Three years after his death, Joey Harrow, a musician who lives near to the Dakota Building, and a friend, Amanda Moores, claimed they saw John's ghost near the entrance to the Dakota where he was shot. Harrow said he was "surrounded by an eerie light." Moores added: "I wanted to go up and talk to him, but something in the way he looked at me said no."

Psychic Shawn Robbins said she saw John's ghost in the building and Yoko Ono was reported to have seen John sitting at his white piano. He turned to her and said, "Don't be afraid. I am still with you."

The Dakota has a long history of paranormal activity. Lennon himself said he encountered the apparition of a woman walking down the long halls of the building. He named her the Crying Lady Ghost. Other celebrities and notable figures who have lived in that building have also had very similar experienced. Maury Povich described the building as "very haunted."

In 1965, three men repainting the walls and re-varnishing woodwork in an apartment felt they were being watched. One saw a ghost of a boy of about ten years old dressed in a Buster Brown suit, a style of the early 1900s. A musty odor accompanied the apparition. The three also saw a ghost that had the body of a male in his 20s and a face of a young child. After the job was done, one of the painters was doing some touch-up work in a large closet when suddenly the door slammed and the light went out. He groped his way off the ladder, propped the door open and turned the light back on. Something grabbed his arm and pushed it against the light bulb.

Several years later, reports surfaced of a little girl in turn-of-the-century clothing who appeared to painters working in the building. This little girl seems to be the most frequently witnessed apparition and is always friendly, often smiling at people, and approaching them as if to greet them.

Apparently some tenants like the Dakota so much that they never want to leave.

THE QUEEN MARY

The retired ocean liner was nicknamed the Gray Ghost during World War II when it ferried soldiers across the Atlantic. But it wasn't until after it was permanently docked in Long Island, California and became a hotel that the ghosts made themselves known. Mysterious noises reported include the sound of crying children in a nursery room and a splashing noise in a drained swimming pool.

In 1966, the year before the ocean liner was decommissioned after 31 years of service, 18-year-old John Pedder, an engineer, was crushed by a watertight door in the engine room during a fire drill. His ghost is said to haunt the ship.

The ship-hotel, now a tourist attraction, includes restaurants and a museum, but not necessarily a sound night's sleep! One of the most haunted spots of the ship is Cabin B340, which is no longer rented out due to extensive paranormal activity. It's believed that an eight-year-old girl was murdered in the cabin.

The spirit of a young girl named Jackie Korin, who drowned in the second-class pool, supposedly haunts the first-class pool, and she's not alone. A young woman by the name of Sarah, who was said to have been murdered in the first class women's changing rooms, supposedly haunts the first-class pool with Jackie. Some visitors say they have seen women wearing early 1930s bathing suits in the pool areas, and even seen wet footprints near the empty pool.

It is also said that men screaming and the sound of metal crushing against metal can be heard below decks at the extreme front end of the bow. It's speculated that the screams emanate from ghosts of the sailors aboard the Curacoa at the moment the light cruiser was split in half by the liner.

THE WHITE HOUSE

1600 Pennsylvania Avenue is probably the most famous address in the U.S. It's also inhabited by a multitude of ghosts from its long history. Presidents, first ladies, White House staff members and guests have reported ghostly encounters.

In the early 1860s, First Lady Mary Todd Lincoln, who believed in spiritualism, reportedly held séances in the White House to commune with the spirits of her dead sons. It's not clear whether or not she made contact, but she told friends she had heard Andrew Jackson stomping and swearing through the halls of the presidential residence. The Rose Room, Jackson's bedchamber while he was president, is believed by some to be one of the most haunted rooms in the White House.

Before long, the first lady's husband, would also haunt the White House. In fact, Abraham Lincoln is reportedly the most sighted ghost in the White House. First Lady Eleanor Roosevelt used the Lincoln Bedroom as her study, and sensed his presence when she worked there late at night. During her visit to the White House, Queen Wilhelmina of the Netherlands reportedly feinted after she saw Lincoln's ghost, complete with top hat. British Prime Minister Winston Churchill, on a visit to the White House, told a story of emerging naked from his evening bath smoking his customary cigar, only to find a ghostly

Lincoln sitting by the fireplace in his room.

More recently, Jenna Bush, daughter of George W., claims she encountered ghosts in the White House. Supposedly, music from the 1920s also emanated from the fireplace in her bedroom. One night after hearing such music, Jenna ran into her twin sister's room and told her about it. The next night, Barbara stayed in the room and heard the same music.

Maybe a sleepover for congressional leaders in in order. Lincoln just might spook the do-nothing Congress into action!

AMITYVILLE HORROR HOUSE

Christopher Lutz grew up in what is often referred to as "the most haunted house in America." But after a string of movies and books, a more accurate description would be "the most commercialized haunted house in America." After decades of avoiding publicity, Lutz began talking about his memories of the house in Amityville, New York on Long Island in November 2011.

The house first attracted attention in 1974 when 23-year-old Ronald DeFeo returned from a night of drinking and shot his parents and four younger siblings. He claimed voices told him to do it.

Just over a year later, the Lutz family purchased the house and moved in. However, they lasted only 28 days before they abandoned the house, claiming it was possessed by demons. Because of numerous contradictions and inaccuracies, the horrifying events that supposedly occurred in the famed house have been labeled a hoax by skeptical investigators.

However, Christopher Lutz, speaking to a reporter for a local Fox News station in Phoenix, said that he remains disturbed by a chilling series of incidents that took place in the house. But he's just as upset by the way Hollywood has spun the story.

While strange things occurred in the house, Lutz said that many of the events portrayed in the Amityville Horror movie were made up. For example, there was no demon that took the form of a giant pig. The book, Amityville Horror, by Jay Anson exaggerated the facts, and once in the hands of Hollywood accuracy no longer mattered.

Lutz is well aware that some investigators contend the entire story was made up by George Lutz, his stepfather. Yet, the younger Lutz maintained that unexplained phenomena occurred in the house and terrified him. "An apparition manifested just outside my bedroom door. It scared the crap out of me as a little kid."

While the mass murder in the house was portrayed as the source of the hauntings, Lutz noted that his stepfather dabbled in the occult and recited the names of demons after the family moved into the home. "Had he done that in any other house it wouldn't have been an issue. But to do it in that house…that's what triggered events there."

BROWN LADY OF RAYNHAM HALL

She reportedly haunts Raynham Hall, a 400-year-old country estate in Norfolk, England. The haunting attracted international attention when the image of the 'Brown Lady' appeared on a photograph of a stairway, taken by a photographer for Country Life Magazine in 1936. It became one of the most famous paranormal photographs of all time. She is called the Brown Lady because of the brown brocade dress she appears to wear.

According to legend, the Brown Lady is the ghost of Lady Dorothy Walpole (1686—1726), second wife of Charles 'Turnip' Townshend, who was notorious for his violent temper. Supposedly, Townshend discovered that his wife had committed adultery with Lord Wharton so he punished her by locking her in her rooms in Raynham Hall. She remained there until her death in 1726.

But if residents of Raynham Hall are right, Dorothy is still trapped in the country estate. A long penance, it seems, for her affair.

TOP TEN HAUNTED PLACES

1) Myrtle Plantation—St. Francisville, LA
2) La Laurie Mansion—New Orleans
3) Eastern State Penitentiary - Philadelphia
4) Waverly Hills Sanatorium—Louisville, KY
5) Raynham Hall—Norfolk, England
6) The White House—Washington, D.C.
7) The Stanley Hotel—Estes Park, Colorado
8) The Queen Mary—docked at Long Beach
9) Winchester House—San Jose, CA
10) Amityville Horror House—Amityville, N.Y.

2

PHANTOM SHIPS

There are haunted ships, like the Queen Mary, docked in Long Island, California, and then there are phantom ships—vessels that appear at sea and fade away, like ghosts. Just as ghosts are considered a non-material afterlife aspect of a person who has died, phantom ships are the non-physical forms of crafts that once sailed the high seas. Such specters of the sea have been reported for centuries.

Do such fantasmic vessels really exist or are they just optical illusions created by the watery environment and long days, weeks and months at sea? Certainly, some sightings are mirages, created by the refraction of light, mist, and fog. Witnesses, captivated by the power and mystery of the sea, might dredge up legends from the past to explain what they saw.

Yet, veteran mariners and sea captains, whose livelihood is based on their ability to observe and judge, have reported seeing phantom vessels. Such impeccable witnesses, it seems, would recognize a mirage. Because there have been so many sightings, including many with multiple witnesses, clearly these purported vessels are a mystery of the sea that remains unresolved.

THE FLYING DUTCHMAN

Without a doubt, The Flying Dutchman is the best known and one of the most witnessed phantom ships. According to legend, a 17th century Dutch sea captain was caught in a horrific storm off the Cape of Good Hope. The first version of the legend was published in Blackwood's Edinburgh Magazine in May 1821.

Supposedly, the captain refused to anchor in a safe harbor and headed out to sea. As the storm picked up strength, he cursed the wind and vowed to sail the seas forever if he couldn't survive the oncoming storm. The ship was lost at sea that night, and the captain was condemned to relive his terrifying experience throughout eternity.

Veteran U-boat commanders and naval officers are among those who have reported the apparition in the 19th and 20th centuries. The ship usually appears to be glowing with a ghostly illumination. After Prince George of Wales, the future King George V, saw the phantom vessel, his tutor Dalton wrote about the sighting.

At 4 a.m. the Flying Dutchman crossed our bows. A strange red light as of a phantom ship all aglow, in the midst of which light the masts, spars and sails of a brig 200 yards distant stood out in strong relief as she came up on the port bow, where also the officer of the watch from the bridge clearly saw her, as did the quarterdeck midshipman, who was sent forward at once to the forecastle; but on arriving there was no vestige nor any sign whatever of any material ship was to be seen either near or right away to the horizon, the night being clear and the sea calm

The legend has been retold in various forms from a Wagner opera to literary references to a cartoon and movies, including a reference in Pirates of the Caribbean.

The Flying Dutchman may be the single most well known ghost ship, but we can't forget the Bermuda Triangle and its mysterious history of disappearances and ghost ships.

THE BERMUDA TRIANGLE

Since the arrival of Columbus to the New World, unusual phenomena has been recorded in the area of the Atlantic referred to as the Bermuda Triangle. It wasn't until 1950, though, when the triangle started to take shape. That's when an article by E.V.W Jones of the Associated Press described mysterious disappearances of ships and aircraft between the Florida coast and Bermuda beginning in the late '40s.

Two years later, an article by George X. Sand in *Fate* Magazine recounted a "series of strange marine disappearances, each leaving no trace whatever, that have taken place in the past few years" in a "watery triangle bounded roughly by Florida, Bermuda and Puerto Rico." Then, in 1964, an article by Vincent Gaddis in the February issue of Argosy coined the term 'Bermuda Triangle.' The following year he used it again in his book, Invisible Horizons. The phrase took hold, even though the mysterious happenings at sea were never limited to those boundaries.

While you've probably heard stories of missing vessels and aircrafts, you might not know about the ghosts of the Bermuda Triangle. Here we move into the realm of folklore, some of it created by the tabloid press. While many of their most dramatic stories about the Bermuda Triangle are impossible to confirm—probably for good reason—they definitely stretch our imaginations.

Listen to these accounts, which were published in the *Weekly World News*. On November 6, 2001, about a month after the building housing the publication became the first target of the anthrax attack, the tabloid offered up tales from the Devil's Triangle—another moniker for the mysterious region—to distract us from the distressing events of the latter months of that year.

SPIRITS AT SEA

Take the story of Shannon Bracy, a forty-two-year-old nurse from New Zealand who supposedly came face-to-face with the spirits of airmen and seamen wandering about in the limbo of the Devil's Triangle. On the last leg of a sailing adventure from Christchurch, New Zealand, to Bermuda, she was entering her noon position in the log when suddenly she noticed a fog settling in around her vessel. Within a couple of minutes, everything had turned stark white.

"Suddenly, I wasn't on my boat anymore. It was like I was in an eerie, desolate void. Then the spirits came. I saw men in seamen's dress and men in uniforms with wings on their flight jackets. I saw other men and women, too, even little children. They were all lifeless, drifting beings with expressions of great pain and sorrow on their faces."

Shannon cried out for help, begging God to save her, and then she found herself back in the cockpit of her sloop. But now it was near midnight and she'd lost twelve hours. "People have told me that it was all just a terrible dream, but I don't think so," she said in a story first published in the *Australian World Adventures* Magazine.

THE UNDEAD CAPTAIN

Then there's the even more peculiar tale from Weekly World News involving Captain Barney Spooner, the skipper of the trawler Matilda II. After Spooner apparently suffered a heart attack and died, his wife and sons decided to abide by his longstanding wish to be buried at sea.

They wrapped him in a blanket, tied an anchor around the body, and threw him overboard. But, according to the account, in a feat that would make Houdini envious, Spooner turned up alive three days later. His family and the crew of the *Matilda II* spotted him floating near the vessel, and one of his sons pulled him aboard a dinghy.

"There was no doubt in our minds that Dad died," son Jonathan said. "He just keeled over and that was it. He had no heartbeat, no pulse, and no breathing."

Spooner said he awakened into a mysterious, alien world. "I saw them all…every one of those ships and planes that had been swallowed up in the Devil's Triangle. I saw the lost ships—the *Cyclops, the Marine Sulphur Queen*, the *Raifuku Maru*, and *Witchcraft*. And I saw the planes—the five Navy Avengers, the *Star Tiger*, and so many other planes. They were everywhere.…And I saw the faces of all the people who had vanished. They drifted past me like a slow-motion film. They had no expressions on their faces. They were just images frozen in time."

In those two stories, the Bermuda Triangle becomes the equivalent of the underworld of mythology, a mournful abode of lost wandering souls, who are mere pale reflections of their former personalities. While the Gulf Stream flows through the Bermuda Triangle, Acheron, the river of affliction, and Cocytus, the river of lamentation, flow through the underworld of the Greek myths.

The famed Triangle is both real and otherworldly. It's a place where extraordinary things happen; it's a popular urban legend, and it's an archetype, a model from our collective unconscious that has a life of its own.

THE LAKE MICHIGAN TRIANGLE

The whole lake is full of ghost stories," says author and historian Ursula Bielski. She and her husband, David Cowan, who operate Chicago Hauntings, contend that there is a triangle in Lake Michigan between Chicago, Manitowoc and Ludington similar to the Bermuda Triangle. "People report seeing ghost ships, and boaters have picked up people from the water who say their ship sunk, and then the people disappear."

ROUSE SIMMONS

The *Rouse Simmons* transported cargos of Christmas trees year after year across Lake Michigan at the beginning of the 20th century. It was known as the Christmas tree ship, because it's captain and owner, Herman Schuenemann, sold the trees directly to Chicago families right at the dock and offered the best prices. In 1912, the three-masted schooner disappeared in a storm, but many sailors would report seeing the ghost ship in the years following the disaster.

In the Christmas spirit, Schuenemann dressed the main mast of the schooner with electric Christmas decorations so people could identify his vessel when it arrived dockside at the Clark Street bridge. He was affectionately known as 'Captain Santa' because he gave away some of the trees to needy families. The rest he sold for between fifty cents and a dollar apiece.

In late November of 1912, Schuenemann loaded the schooner with 5,500 trees from Thompson Harbor near Manistique, Michigan and planned to make the week-long journey to Chicago. Difficult weather with snow covering the tree farms in Michigan and Wisconsin discouraged his competitors from making their own journeys. So Captain Schuenemann hoped to make a large profit. However, the storm turned into a deadly gale with 60 mph winds, and the ship was overweight with the mass of sodden trees gathering ice.

When the Kewaunee Life Saving Station spotted the *Rouse Simmons* on Nov. 23, it was low in the water with tattered sails, flying its flag at half-mast to signal that it was in distress. Logs from the station show that a surfman spotted the *Simmons* at 2:50 p.m. and alerted the station keeper. He telephoned the nearest station, located just south of Kewaunee, which sent out a power boat on a rescue mission to save the crew. But the Simmons had vanished.

A few days later, all hope was lost as bits of the *Rouse Simmons* began to wash up on shore, including a note stuffed inside a bottle corked with a small piece of pine cut from one of the Christmas trees. It read:

Friday…everybody goodbye. I guess we are all through. During the night the small boat washed overboard. Leaking bad. Ivald and Steve lost too. God help us.

In 1924, Captain Schuenemann's wallet, still wrapped in protective oilskin, was discovered in the net of a fishing boat. Then in 1971, a salvage diver discovered the remains of the *Rouse Simmons*, her hold still filled with Christmas trees, resting in 172 feet of water.

Since shortly after her fateful final voyage, Great Lakes sailors have reported seeing the ghost of the *Rouse Simmons*. She's most often spotted on moonlit nights, her sails ripped to tatters and wildly flapping about as if blown by gale winds, as she and her phantom crew continue in desperation to reach safety. Sailors claim one moment she is there, and the next moment she has vanished.

"There is a long history of anomalous phenomena in Lake Michigan," according to author and publisher Kathy Doore, of West Palm Beach. Doore remembered a time in July 1978, when she was with a fleet of antique sailboats on the lake. "It was a clear night, but a sudden, dense fog rushed in and enveloped us. The boats began steering themselves in circles, completing 360-degree pirouettes."

During the time the boats were engulfed in the fog, Doore says she saw her father, who had recently died, on the deck and was able to talk with him. The event changed her life. When the fog lifted, Doore and her friends were unable to account for several hours of missing time. After she wrote about the experience and Discovery Channel did a feature on it, she began receiving letters from Chicagoans reporting similar spooky events on the lake.

Notes Frederick Stonehouse, author of *Haunted Lake Michigan*, "Lake Michigan is chock full of things that go splash in the night."

TS KØBENHAVN

A Danish five-masted barque, the København was used as a naval training vessel until its disappearance after December 22, 1928. Built by the Danish East Asiatic Company in 1921, it was the world's largest sailing ship at the time.

The ship was en route from Buenos Aires to Australia when it disappeared. A lengthy search failed to turn up any trace of the

København. The disappearance has become one of the greatest maritime mysteries of the modern era, and led to considerable speculation about the ship's ultimate fate. That's especially true because a ship fitting its description was sighted numerous times in the South Pacific during the two years after its disappearance. In July 1930, the crew of an Argentine freighter sighted a five-masted "phantom ship" during a gale. The captain logged their statements and wondered if this was the "wraith of the Copenhagen." Additional sightings came in the following weeks from Easter Island and the Peruvian coast.

In 1934, *The New York Times* reported that a *København* cadet's diary had been found in a bottle on Bouvet Island in the South Atlantic. The supposed diary indicated that the ship had been destroyed by icebergs and abandoned, the crew abandoned the ship in lifeboats. In 1935, human remains and the wreckage of a lifeboat were found partly buried in the sand along the southwest coast of Africa. These may have come from the *København*.

HMS EURYDICE

A 26-gun Royal Navy corvette, the Eurydice sank in 1878 after crossing the Atlantic from Bermuda, taking the lives of all 300 sailors aboard. The loss occurred in a fierce snowstorm off the Isle of Wight and is considered one of Britain's worst peacetime naval disasters. Among the witnesses was a young Winston Churchill who watched the ship capsize from a cliff on the Isle of Wight.

Sailors have frequently sighted the phantom ship over the years. Commander F. Lipscomb of a royal naval submarine reported taking evasive action to avoid the ship only to find that the ship had disappeared.

Prince Edward of England was filming a segment of his TV series, *Crown and Country*, on the Isle of Wight on Oct. 17, 1998 when he witnessed the ghost ship.

"We were talking about a ghost ship on the Isle of Wight and how we could illustrate this three-masted schooner that just disappears. Suddenly someone said, 'Look, there's one now,' and sure enough out to sea there was a three-masted schooner. Someone said, 'We'll wait until it gets a little closer to the shoreline' and then someone else said, 'Where's it gone? ' We looked and it had disappeared."

SS TRICOLOR

The Norwegian merchant vessel was hauling a load of chemicals in her hull when she caught fire and exploded on January 5, 1931 near Sri Lanka. The vessel had encountered a severe tropical storm during her fateful journey, and possibly a lightning strike started the fire. A French liner, the S.S. Porthos, witnessed the destruction of the ship and responded to the distress call.

Five years to the day after the Tricolor's demise, a British freighter, the *S.S. Khosuru*, sailed in the same waters and encountered a derelict vessel that seemed devoid of a crew. The ship passed close enough to the *Khosuru* for crew members to read the name of the vessel from her hull—the *Tricolor*. Before the crew could overtake the vessel, a torrential rain blocked all visibility. Five minutes later, when the rain let up, the derelict was nowhere in sight. Only later the captain of the *Khosuru* discovered that the position he had seen the strange ship was the exact place where the Tricolor exploded and sank.

YOUNG TEAZER

Privateer vessels, like the Young Teazer, were sailing vessels authorized by the government to attack foreign ships during time of war. An American privateer schooner, the Teazer was remarkably fast and repeatedly attacked British vessels off the coast of Halifax during the War of 1812. But its days were numbered.

In June 1813, the *Teazer* eluded the Nova Scotian privateer brig Sir John Sherbrooke, escaping into the fog. Shortly after the *HMS La Hogue* headed into Mahone Bay. With nightfall pending, the *La Hogue* was joined by the *HMS Orpheus* and the crews prepared to board *Teazer*, which had nowhere left to run.

The *La Hogue* sent five boats, but as they approached the schooner, the *Young Teazer* exploded. Seven of the crew survived and claimed that just before the explosion, they last saw one of the ship's officers running to the main magazine with flaming embers.

A year after the tragedy, the phantom ship reportedly entered the same waters where it had exploded. As it came nearer witnesses recognized the spectral vessel as the privateer, and then it vanished in a cloud of flame and smoke. The story spread throughout the country, and on the next anniversary many more were on hand, watching for 'the fire ship.' Supposedly, the ghost ship made another appearance, and again disappeared in flames.

Locals in Mahone Bay, Nova Scotia say that on foggy nights near the full moon, spectral light can be seen in the bay. They are known as 'The Teazer Light.'

THE CALEUCHE

While the Flying Dutchman is undoubted the best known phantom ship tale, probably the most interesting one is a phantom vessel that sails the seas near the island of Chiloe in southern Chile. Not only are there numerous stories of sightings, but the Caleuche's crew of foreign men dressed in black reportedly terrorize and abduct islanders. To the islanders, the Caleuche's crew are brujos, or witches, capable of magical deeds, such as shape-shifting into animals. In fact, the name Caleuche comes from Mapudungun, a native American language. Caleutum means to transform or change state, and che means people or person.

One night in 1968, Aaron Garcia Gonzalez, a pastor in Ancud, was startled to see a large sailing vessel enter the shallow waters of the Rio Pudeto. "I saw several brilliant lights, then a mast, then two more masts and finally, a ship illuminated in brilliant colors." Father Garcia watched the ship for half an hour before it faded away in the same slow manner that it had materialized.

Most of the stories about the ghost ship come from the mid to late 20th century and were recorded by Chilean writer Antonio Cardenas Tabies, who encountered the phantom ship while aboard a rowboat one night with four others. According to his story, Tabies and his friends had rowed into a thick fog when a small launch passed within a few feet of their boat. They never saw anyone on board or heard any noise from the motor. The men continued rowing toward shore, but couldn't reach land. In the morning, they found themselves in the same place they had been when they entered the fog.

Tabies believes that the launch was the *Caleuche* in one of its altered forms, and when they crossed paths with it, the crew of *brujos* cast a spell on them. Possibly they were abducted, but have no memory of what happened. That might account for why they found themselves in the same place the next morning.

Many of the stories Tabies recorded deal with the abduction of islanders by the crew. One man, who was supposedly taken at the age of 18, returned to his village 50 years later. When questioned, he simply said he had been on a boat and begged his brother not to ask anything more about it.

Elena Vera Guerrero of Ancud met the man. "I was visiting Marcelino Saldivia, a friend who lives in another village, and took offense at the strange behavior of one of the men present. He didn't bother to say hello, practically never spoke, and seemed so remote he might as well not have been there."

Saldivia told her the man was his brother, who had disappeared half a century ago while sleeping on the porch. During Easter week 1976, Saldivia was feeling nostalgic about his brother and visited their old home on the banks of the Rio Pudeto. There, seated in the living room and dressed in the same clothes he'd worn as a young man, was his brother, now old and evidently demented.

Tabies is baffled by the stories he collected about the *Caleuche*, but he's certain that it exists. "There are two types of mysteries: those which are accounts of experiences which have occurred and cannot be explained, and those born of the history of a people. The *Caleuche* is a mystery of both kinds."

3

LEGENDARY GHOSTS, MYSTICAL BEINGS

Just as the story of the ghost ship Caleuche is a part of the cultural heritage on the Chilean island of Chiloe, legendary ghosts and ghost-like beings are a part of cultures and folklore around the world. They range from shape-shifting beings and hungry ghosts to horrendous monsters and bizarre creatures from the underworld. Are they simply tall tales, or are there nuggets of truth behind these tales?

CURI, PERU

In the highlands of Peru, the peasants tell of a malevolent being called the Curi that haunts travelers and locals alike, especially those hiking in the Andes.

Edy, a Peruvian tourist guide, had an experience with Curi a few years ago, on November 1, All Soul's Day in Peru. She had ascended a trail to a mesa and was looking for another guide, Juan, who had gone ahead with lanterns for the campsite. Edy's group was following her and she could hear them, but couldn't see them because of a mound of large rocks behind her.

Then she saw Juan sitting on a boulder. He called out to her, urging her to join him. She began walking toward him but realized something was wrong. He had gone ahead of her, but now he was behind her, and he hadn't passed her on the trail. As she moved closer, she saw that he had a whip in his hand and suddenly he floated straight into the air.

Juan had once told her if she ever saw such a thing she should walk away and focus her intent on divine light. None of the others on the trail saw the being with the exception of one woman, who was a medium. They continued their climb to the mesa and found

Juan waiting for them. He was unaware of the entity that had taken on his appearance.

"When we returned to the village, the peasants told us that the Curi takes on different shapes and that November 1 is not a good time to climb to the mesa, because the Curi is present."

On another occasion, Edy recalls making the same climb with a burro, but the animal became nervous and refused to move. Repeatedly, when she tried to walk the burro along the trail, the animal pulled away. As she sat down to wait for her companions, an old man in a black hat came along and Edy saluted him in the custom of the village. But the man didn't respond and continued on. Looking closer, she realized that he was floating above the ground.

"I began to feel drowsy and heard a buzzing noise. Then suddenly Juan was calling me frantically." As he reached her, he said that as he turned the bend in the trail, he saw a very large man, who he thought was a brujo or witch, standing next to her. But she had seen no such man.

DJINN, THE ARABIAN PENINSULA

The story of Aladdin and the magic lamp from the tales of the Arabian Nights is well known. Aladdin rubs the dust off the ancient lamp and a Genie appears in a cloud of smoke. But the Genie is a benevolent version of the Djinn, pronounced 'jinn' with a silent 'd,' a race of beings from Arabic mythology that can be either good or evil. The word djinn comes from the Arabic "jinni," or demon. Its root is janna, meaning "to cover or conceal." In English, the word is often translated as "genie."

They are a race of master shape-shifters, who exist in a dimension parallel to ours. They disguise themselves in the form of a variety of beings in order to keep their true identities hidden.

While these powerful beings are little known in the West, with the exception of the Genie in the bottle story, believers in the djinns are found throughout the Arabian Peninsula and Central Asia. They are even mentioned in the Koran. In fact, Satan often is believed to be the most prominent of the djinns. Supposedly, the djinns preceded humans and were made from fire, while humans were made from clay, and angels from light.

While the djinn are ancient, they supposedly are still active. According to one recent story, a man was walking along the beach in the United Arab Emirates and found a hijab, the headscarf Muslim women wear. He picked it up and took it home. After that, he was possessed by a djinn. Witnesses claimed he spoke in a strange voice and said he was a thousand years old. During an exorcism of the man, the djinn was asked why he took the man's body. The ancient entity replied that he was attracted to his eyes. As they say, the eyes are the doorway to the soul.

THE JIKININKI, JAPAN

These beings from Japanese mythology are known as human-eating ghosts, or hungry ghosts who have insatiably appetites for corpses. The Jikininki are said to be the spirits of selfish humans who are doomed to an after-life existence of munching on the dead. These entities appear human-like with rotting flesh, bright eyes and claws. They're so frightening that just glimpsing one can leave a person frozen in fear, unable to flee.

LESHY, EASTERN EUROPE

Known as guardians of the forests, the Leshy hate humans. They look like humans, but can grow and shrink in size. They also prefer the company of bears over mankind. The Leshies supposedly hide axes from lumberjacks, hence helping to preserve the forest. The evil version of this species is capable of mimicking voices of friends or family members in order to catch the attention of their targets. They lead their victims into a cave, and then, oddly enough, tickle them to death. What a way to go!

Here's the good news. It's possible to escape the giddy whims of the Leshy by turning your clothes inside out and wearing your shoes on the wrong feet.

FINFOLK, ORKNEY ISLANDS, SCOTLAND

The Finfolk of Orkney folklore were a race of dark and gloomy sorcerers, who greatly feared by humans. While their abode was the undersea world, they were skilled mariners, had power over storms, and were shapeshifters, who came ashore whenever they wanted to terrorize islanders. They wintered in Finfolkaheem, a majestic city at the bottom of the sea. In the summer, they took up residence on their magical island home of Hildaland that appeared and disappeared.

The Finfolk were known for abducting humans and taking their captives to their hidden island homes. Usually, the abductees never escaped, and became the wife or husband of Finfolk. It's thought that the mean-spirited influence of the Finfolk was a way of explaining the many disappearances and death at sea. Interestingly, it' said that the Finfolk disappeared with the arrival of Christianity.

KELPIE & SELKIE, SCOTLAND

The legendary Kelpie is a shape-shifting water horse that haunts the rivers and streams of Scotland. While it can take many forms, the Kelpie is said to often appear as a beautiful tame horse standing by a river in order to entice unwary travelers. But anyone mounting the horse would quickly be submerged, drowned, and gobbled up by the creature.

The Kelpie was takes on the form of a hairy humanoid, who leaps out from the riverside vegetation to attack passing travellers. Once caught in its grip, there is no escape as the creature crushes the life out of its prey. One Kelpie is recorded as being banished by St. Columba from the River Ness, resulting in the Kelpie being associated with the Loch Ness Monster.

According to James Mackinley, author of *Folklore of Scottish Lochs and Springs* (1893), the Kelpie's power of shape shifting resides in its bridle, and anyone who can take control of the bridle can tame the creature and put it to work. A Kelpie had the strength of at least ten horses and the endurance of many more. However, the fairy races were typically dangerous in captivity. It was said that the MacGregor clan possesses a Kelpies bridle, passed down through the generations from when one of their clan managed to save himself from a Kelpie near Loch Slochd.

The mythical Selkies were creatures that could transform themselves from seal to human form and back again by removing and replacing their magical seal skins. The Selkie men were renowned for their encounters with human females, and the story could've served as a way of explaining pregnancies out of wedlock and illicit affairs.

One well known tale deals with a man who found a beautiful female Selkie sunbathing on a beach. He stole her skin and forced her to become his wife and bear his children. Years later, she found her skin and escaped back to her seal form and the sea. Such a tale could explain why a wife abandoned her family. She found her skin! Interestingly, the Selkie tale parallels the stories of shapeshifting dolphins from Brazil. See below.

BEAN NIGHE, SCOTLAND

These bizarre ghosties are creatures from the Celtic Otherworld sent to this world on a cleaning mission related to people who are about to die. The Bean Nighe are said to be the spirits of women who died while giving birth. Their task: to launder the bloody garments of people who are near death, especially women dying in childbirth.

DOMOVOI, RUSSIA

Keep an eye out for a small bearded man running around your house. According to Russian folklore, these domestic ghouls can be found in every home. The Domovoi are talented shape-shifters, who can disguise themselves as housemates, family members, friends or pets. Whether a Domovoi is good or evil is up to you. If you curse frequently, he'll treat you poorly. But if you live a clean life, he'll be nice. But watch out, the Domovoi might steal your socks, only one of each pair, of course.

That sounds like the black hole inside your family's washing machine, where socks and other articles of clothing mysteriously disappear.

ENCANTADO, BRAZIL

These mystical creatures are stunningly attractive, well dressed, and party-ready. Encantados are musically inclined shape-shifting dolphins, who emerge from their underwater abodes to impregnate human party-goers. They often wear hats to hide their blowholes, because their natural form is that of dolphins.

Encantados sometimes abduct their victims and carry them back to their Encante. For this reason, *Riverenos*, the locals who live in towns along the Amazon, are often wary of the river. So if dolphins look like they're smiling, now you know why!

CHICKCHARNEES & LUSCAS, ANDROS ISLAND, THE BAHAMAS

Chickcharnees are large bird-like creatures that are either furry or feathered with mystical powers. They resemble oversized owls, stand about three-feet tall and live in pine forests. According to legend, if a traveler meets a chickcharney and treats it well, he or she will be rewarded with good luck. But, treating a chickcharney badly will result in tough luck and hard times. According to the locals, the chickcharney are still occasionally spotted in the forest.

It should be noted that people who claim they were abducted by small gray alien beings sometimes say they thought they were looking at owls when they first saw the beings. They also say that the Grays seem to possess mystical abilities to move through walls, levitate, read minds and communicate telepathically.

Combine that bit of information with the fact that Andros Island is the home of a secret American naval base that has been called the 'Underwater Area 51,' and the mystery of the chickcharney deepens. Most of the base, known as the Atlantic Underwater Testing and Evaluation Center (AUTEC), is located underwater in the Tongue of the Ocean, a trough in the sea that drops off to more than six miles in depth.

Underwater UFOs, which rise out of the sea and dive back into it, have been sighted here on numerous occasions, and some of them reportedly are enormous, more than a mile in diameter. Could the little Grays be living in the depths spying on the military base that might be spying on them? It's all conjecture, but it makes for fascinating stories.

The other mysterious creature on Andros Island, the lusca, supposedly resides in the blue holes in and around the island. Resembling a giant octopus, the Lusca is said to span two hundred feet with tentacles extending seventy-five feet from its body. That's just one description, though. It's also been called a multi-headed monster, a dragon-like creature, or an evil spirit. Take your pick.

4

FAMOUSLY HAUNTED

Some famous people readily say that they've seen ghosts. Others who were famous and are now legendary, are ghosts, or so witnesses report. To call the latter 'famous ghosts,' however, would be a misnomer. It's not the ghosts who are famous, but the people they were.

They lived exalted lives and were so successful, so attached to the physical world, that possibly a part of them remains here with us, making guest appearances from time to time. Or, more appropriately, *ghost* appearances, usually in their favorite haunts—wherever they felt most at home.

There's an interesting pattern with ghosts of the famous. Many were icons. Marilyn Monroe was the sex goddess of her era. George Reeves was the original superman. Rudolf Valentino was the premiere heartthrob. Orson Welles made a deep impression on Hollywood as a writer, director, and actor, and Harry Houdini was the archetypal magician. Then there was Lucy.

LUCILLE BALL

The famous comedian-actress starred in films, as well as I Love Lucy, one of the best-known TV shows of all time. Ball was 77 years old when she died on April 26, 1989 during surgery. The ghost of Lucy reportedly haunts her former home at 100 North Roxbury Drive in Beverly Hills, California. According to accounts, puzzling and unexplained happenings have repeatedly occurred at the home. They include windows breaking for no known reason, haunting voices heard, and furniture and other items mysteriously moved about the house.

As Ricky Ricardo used to say: Lucy, you've got 'splainin' to do!

MARILYN MONROE

She died of an overdose of sleeping pills on August 5, 1962, and today her ghost is said to materialize in the Brentwood house where she died. Does Marilyn wander the premises, wondering what happened?

A full-length mirror that was removed from her house is located at the Hollywood Roosevelt Hotel, where Marilyn stayed at the height of her career. Now patrons occasionally glimpse her image in the mirror located in the hotel's lobby.

Another location where Marilyn's ghost has been spotted is at her burial site at the Westwood Memorial Cemetery. Maybe her continued popularity has kept her close to the Earth plane where she can still see herself on the classic film channel.

GEORGE REEVES

The original Superman, the legendary actor died under mysterious circumstances, and the appearance of his ghost suggests there was more involved in his death than we know. Multiple sightings have been reported from the Benedict Canyon Drive home where he died in 1959 from an apparent self-inflicted gunshot wound. Visitors to the home have either reported hearing strange gunshots and screams or seeing a full apparition of Reeves in his Superman costume.

LIBERACE

Walter Valentino Liberace, simply known as "Liberace" by his adoring fans, died on February 4, 1987 at the age of 68. Liberace was known for his remarkable piano talents, and his way of dazzling his audiences with his numerous diamond rings.

Since his death, Liberace's ghost has been reported at Carluccio's Tivoli Gardens. He had owned the restaurant, and had a private lounge there where he entertained his dearest friends. The mysterious happenings linked to the ghost include bottles that fall over, restroom doors that mysteriously lock and unlock, and unexplained power outages. One year on May 16, the electricity at the restaurant shut down, and nothing could be found wrong with it. Finally, one of the staff realized it was Liberace's birthday, and wished him a happy birthday. Instantly, the power was restored.

HARRY HOUDINI

Nearly 90 years after his death, Harry Houdini remains one of the best-known escape artists and magicians of all time. Before he died on October 31, 1926, he promised his wife Bess he would come back from 'the other side' and contact her. Today, the ghost of Harry Houdini reportedly has been seen haunting the property at 2398 Laurel Canyon Boulevard in Hollywood, the site of his house that burned down in 1959.

JOHN LENNON

The ghost of this free spirit has been seen, not only in the Dakota where he lived and was murdered, but all over the world, according to reports. Among witnesses are Liam Gallagher, former front-man for Oasis, and Paul McCartney who saw John while they were recording one of Lennon's unfinished symphonies. Several psychics held a televised séance in 2006 at the Dakota building and other spots around the world seeking to connect with John in the after-life. They claimed Lennon's ghost made more than one appearance. Apparently, he disappointed fans by not bringing along his ghost guitar.

RUDOLF VALENTINO

He rose to stardom in the early years of movies, and is enshrined as the first heartthrob of the silver screen. He died tragically at the age of 31 in 1926 from an infection contracted during an operation. His former Hollywood home, Falcon's Lair, reportedly has been haunted since his death. Actor Harry Carey, who purchased the home, reported seeing a ghostly figure similar to the actor's rugged good looks. Fashion icon Millicent Rogers saw Valentino's ghost once and refused to ever set foot in the house again.

LON CHANEY

He was the original 'creep show' long before Stephen King's Creepshow appeared on film. A master of ghoulish makeup, he was the epitome of horror. His spirit is said to haunt a sound-stage on the Universal Studios Hollywood lot where workers have reported hearing footsteps and seeing a caped man dashing along the catwalks. The stage was used to film part of Chaney's iconic

Phantom of the Opera, and supposedly remains standing because several mysterious accidents have prevented the studio from fully dismantling it.

ORSON WELLES

His brilliant career as a writer, actor and producer ended when he died from a heart attack at the age of 70 on October 10, 1985. Known for his love of fine dining, Wells often ate dinner at a restaurant called Ma Maison, which is now the location of Sweet Lady Jane's Bakery in Los Angeles. Employees have reported seeing a large man dressed in black sitting in a corner table and smelling the sweet scents of cigar smoke and brandy.

GHOST SIGHTINGS BY CELEBS

Kate Hudson

She revealed during the filming of Skeleton Key that she's had her fair share of ghostly encounters. She said she's seen a ghost with no face many times, and she once glimpsed the spirit of her grandmother.

Nicholas Cage

No shortage of ghosts in this celeb actor's life. Cage's favorite spooky encounter occurred when he was visiting Francis Ford Coppola at his house in Napa Valley. He was staying in the attic when late one night a woman with big hair appeared. At first, he thought it was his aunt. But when she approached him, it was a stranger, and a dead one at that. The ghost left him cowering under the covers.

Matthew McConaughey

The popular heartthrob says he lives in a haunted house, and recalls how one night in 2003, he kept hearing the sound of a coin clattering to the floor. He leapt out of bed, snatched a baseball bat, and conducted a naked search for the intruder. The female ghost must've been impressed because McConaughey eventually made peace with her. He calls her Madame Blue.

Telly Savalas

The Kojak star ran out of gas and he was about to start walking when someone with a high-pitched voice asked if he wanted a ride. He turned and saw a guy in a black Cadillac. I thanked him, climbed into the passenger seat, and we drove to the freeway. Savalas had no money with him, but the man loaned him a dollar. He insisted he would pay him back and got him to write his name and address on a scrap of paper.

The next day Savalas called the man. A woman answered and said Harry had been her husband, but he died three years ago. Savalas later met her and recalled, "When I showed her the paper where he'd written his name, she was deeply affected and told him that without a doubt it was her husband's handwriting.

Keanu Reeves

When Keanu was five, he and his sister encountered a ghost in the house where they were living. The ghost wore a white double-breasted suit, but only half of it. The ghost had no legs. Short story; short ghost. Short and kind of creepy!

5

HAUNTED JUSTICE
THE JURY AND THE OUIJA BOARD

Is it possible for murder victims to come back and seek justice for their killers? The justice system doesn't look kindly on testimony from the grave, but on more than one occasion contact with the dead has made its way into the courts.

Take the case of a double murder in England in 1993.

Stephen Young, an insurance broker, was deeply in debt in the winter of 1993 and he knew that newlyweds Harry and Nicola Fuller had lots of cash stored at home. He went to their cottage in Wadhurst, East Sussex on a cold day in February and later said he found the couple dead. But the authorities discovered evidence linking Young to the murders and he was charged with double murder.

On the night of the first day of trial, several jurors decided to undertake their own investigation. After having drinks together, they created a makeshift Ouija board and attempted to contact one of the victims. To their surprise, Harry Fuller joined their party and told them that Young was indeed the murderer. "I was crying by this time, and the other ladies were upset as well," one juror later commented.

The next morning they reported their findings to the other jurors. When the judge found out about the Ouija session, he told the jurors it was not their place to investigate—no matter what the source—and he ordered a mistrial. But later that year, Young was retried and another jury came to the same conclusion as the message received through the Ouija board. Young was found guilty, this time solely by evidence from living witnesses.

A century earlier, the spirit of another murder victim seemingly played a significant role in a trial.

THE GREENBRIER GHOST

On a dreary day in late January of 1897, Mary Jane Heaster watched as her daughter, Zona Heaster Shue, was laid to rest in the cemetery near Greenbrier, West Virginia. The coroner listed the cause of death as complications from childbirth. But Mary Jane knew her 23-year-old daughter had not been giving birth when she died. In fact, as far as anyone knew, Zona wasn't even pregnant. Mary Jane was certain foul play was involved. If only Zona could speak from the grave, she thought, maybe she could find out what happened.

In one of the most remarkable cases on U.S. court records, ghostly communiqués, supposedly from Zona's spirit, helped in convicting her husband, Erasmus Stribbling Trout Shue, of murder. It might be the only case in U.S. history in which testimony purportedly from beyond the grave aided in resolving a crime and convicting the perpetrator.

Just two years before Zona's death, she had given birth to a child out of wedlock, a scandalous event in the late 1800s. The father didn't marry Zona, so the young woman needed a husband. The following year Zona met Erasmus Shue, who went by the name Edward, and a courtship began. He was a new arrival to Greenbrier and planned to open a blacksmith shop.

Mary Jane, however, didn't care for Edward. There was something about him that made her uneasy. It was apparently something Zona couldn't see or intentionally overlooked. Despite her mother's concerns, Zona and Edward married on October 26, 1896.

It didn't take long for Mary Jane's worst fears to materialize. Three months into the marriage, on January 23, 1897, an 11-year-old African-American boy named Andy Jones entered the Shue home and found Zona lying on the floor. He had been sent there by Edward to ask Zona if she needed anything from the market.

The local physician and coroner, Dr. George W. Knapp, arrived at the Shue residence an hour later, and by that time Edward had already taken Zona's lifeless body to an upstairs bedroom. When Knapp entered the room, he was astonished to see that Edward had dressed Zona in her best Sunday clothing - a beautiful dress with a high neck and stiff collar. Edward had also covered her face with a veil.

Knapp tried to examine the body to determine the cause of death, but all the while Edward was weeping and cradling his dead wife's head in his arms. Knapp noticed a slight discoloration on the right side of her cheek and neck. He wanted to examine the marks, but Edward protested so vehemently that Knapp ended the examination, announcing that poor Zona had died of "an everlasting faint." Officially and for the record, he inexplicably wrote that the cause of death was childbirth.

Just as mysterious was his failure to notify the police about the strange marks on her neck that he was unable to examine. Mary Jane had felt that Zona's marriage to Edward would come to a bad end. But she'd never imagined that her daughter would die of some mysterious cause. Her suspicions grew during the wake when Edward acted oddly, not like a husband in mourning. Some of the neighbors at the wake also took notice.

One moment, Edward seemed grief-struck, another moment highly agitated and nervous. He refused to allow anyone near the body. He had placed a pillow on one side of Zona's head and a rolled up cloth on the other, as if keeping her head propped in place. Her neck was covered by a large scarf that Edward claimed was her favorite. At the end of the wake, as the coffin was being prepared to be taken to the cemetery, several people noticed an odd looseness to Zona's head, almost as if it weren't attached to the body.

Despite all of the strangeness surrounding her daughter's death, Mary Jane had no proof of any kind that Edward was somehow to blame for his daughter's death. Her suspicions might have been buried along with Zona had not unexplained phenomena begun to take place.

Mary Jane had taken the rolled up white sheet from Zona's coffin before it was sealed. And now, days after the funeral, she tried to return it to Edward. Still acting peculiar, he refused to take it. Mary Jane brought it back home with her, deciding to keep it in memory of her daughter.

Although the sheet appeared clean, she noticed that it had a peculiar odor. She filled a basin with water in which to wash the sheet, and when she submerged it, the water turned red. Mary Jane stood back in astonishment. She took a pitcher and scooped some of the water from the basin. To her amazement, it was clear. But the white sheet was now stained pink. Mary Jane washed it, boiled it, and hung it in the sun. The stain remained. It was a sign, Mary Jane thought, a message from Zona that her death was far from natural.

Mary Jane prayed every day for weeks, hoping that Zona would somehow reveal the circumstances of her death. Finally her prayers were answered.

Early one evening as winter winds swirled around the streets of Greenbrier, an apparition appeared to Mary Jane. She had just lit her oil lamps and candles, as dusk filled the house, when she maintains Zona's ghost appeared briefly, then returned on three successive days. During these four spectral visits, Mary Jane claimed that Zona told her how she had died.

Edward was cruel and abusive to her, Zona said, and one day his violence went too far. Edward became irrationally angry when she told him she had no meat for dinner. He was overcome with rage and lashed out at his wife. He savagely attacked the defenseless woman and broke her neck. To prove her account, the ghost slowly turned its head completely around at the neck.

Zona's ghost had confirmed her mother's worst suspicions about Edward and his strange behavior at the wake. He had protected Zona's body from close inspection, not because of grief, but because he had murdered the young woman.

Mary Jane told her story to John Preston, the local prosecutor. Preston listened patiently, though skeptically. He had doubts about her story of the telltale ghost, but there was already enough that was suspicious about the case that he decided to re-open it.

Preston ordered Zona's body exhumed for autopsy. Edward Shue protested the action, but had no power to stop it. He began to show signs of stress, and said publicly that he knew he would be arrested, but "they will not be able to prove I did it."

The autopsy revealed that Zona's neck was broken and her windpipe crushed from violent strangulation. Shue was arrested and charged with murder.

As Shue awaited trial, the prosecutor looked into Edward's background and discovered that he had served time in jail for stealing a horse. Shue had been married twice before Zona, and each marriage ended in peculiar ways. His first wife divorced him after he had angrily thrown all of her possessions out of their house.

His second wife wasn't so lucky. She died after a blow to the head, but there was no evidence to pin the death on Shue.

When Mary Jane heard about Edward's past, it confirmed her suspicions about the man. His jailers and cellmates reported that Edward seemed in good spirits while in jail. In fact, he bragged that it was his intention to eventually have seven wives. Since he was only 35 years old, he believed that he could easily realize his ambition. Apparently, he felt certain that he would not be convicted of Zona's death. What evidence was there, after all?

In fact, the evidence against Edward was circumstantial at best. But he didn't count on the testimony of an eyewitness to the murder - Zona.

Edward's trial began in late June. The prosecutor lined up several people to testify against Edward, citing his peculiar behavior and unguarded comments. But would that be enough to convict him? No one could testify that Edward was at or near the scene at the time of Zona's death. Taking the stand in his defense, he vehemently denied the charges.

When the prosecutor attempted to admit Mary Jane's ghostly encounters with Zona as evidence, the judge ruled that testimony from a ghost was inadmissible. But then Edward's defending lawyer made a mistake that perhaps sealed his client's fate. He called Mary Jane to the stand.

In an attempt perhaps to show that the woman was unbalanced, maybe even insane, he brought up the matter of Zona's ghost.

Seated on the witness stand in front of a packed courtroom and an attentive jury, Mary Jane told the story of how Zona's ghost appeared to her and accused Edward of the foul deed. Her neck had been "squeezed off at the first vertebrae."

It's uncertain whether or not the jury took Mary Jane's - or rather Zona's - testimony seriously. But they handed down a verdict of guilty on the charge of murder. Normally, such a conviction would have brought a sentence of death, but because of the circumstantial nature of the evidence, Edward was sentenced to life in prison. He died on March 13, 1900 in the Moundsville, W.V. penitentiary, less than three years after his sentence.

Two questions about the case were never resolved. Was the jury influenced by the story of Zona's ghost? Apparently, no reporters ever asked the jury about their decision. The other question: Was there really a ghost? Maybe Mary Jane Heaster was so convinced that Edward Shue had murdered her daughter that she made up the story to help convict him. Without the ghost story, Edward may never have been brought to trial, and Zona's murder would never have been avenged.

A historical marker near Greenbrier commemorates Zona and the unusual court case related to her death.

INTERRED IN NEARBY CEMETERY IS
ZONA HEASTER SHUE

Her death in 1897 was presumed natural until her spirit appeared to her mother to describe how she was killed by her husband Edward. Autopsy on the exhumed body verified the apparition's account. Edward, found guilty of murder, was sentenced to the state prison. Only known case in which testimony from ghost helped convict a murderer.

LEGALLY HAUNTED

Here's a case where a house was judged legally haunted by a court. Known as *Stambovsky v. Ackley*, the haunted house came under the scrutiny of a New York Supreme Court in 1991. In the decision, the court noted that the owner had previously advertised the house as haunted by ghosts and therefore the purchaser could not rescind the agreement to buy the house on the basis that it was haunted.

Because of its uniqueness, the case has been frequently printed in textbooks on contracts and property law. It is also widely taught in U.S. law school classes and is often cited by other courts.

The house, located in Nyack, New York, was owned by Helen Ackley and members of her family had reported the existence of numerous poltergeists in the house. Ackley herself had reported the existence of ghosts in the house to the *Reader's Digest* and a local newspaper on three occasions between 1977 and 1989. During that period the house was included on a five-house walking tour of the city.

She told reporters about several instances in which the poltergeists interacted directly with members of her family. She claimed that grandchildren received gifts of baby rings, all of which later suddenly disappeared. She also claimed that one ghost would wake her each morning by shaking her bed. She claimed that when spring break arrived she proclaimed loudly that she did not have to wake up early and she would like to sleep in. As a result, her bed did not shake the next morning.

Neither Ackley nor her realtor, Ellis Realty, revealed the haunting to Jeffrey Stambovsky before he entered a contract to purchase the house in 1989 or 1990. Stambovsky made a $32,500 down payment on the agreed price of $650,000. He was from New York City and was not aware of the folklore of Nyack, including the widely known haunting story.

When he learned that the house was supposedly haunted, Stambovsky didn't show up for the closing, which caused him to forfeit the down payment. He then filed an action requesting rescission of the sales contract and for damages for fraudulent misrepresentation by Ackley and Ellis Realty. A New York Supreme Court (trial court) dismissed the action and noted that "as a matter of law, the house is haunted," because of the publicity in national and local publications.

The court also noted that regardless of whether the house was truly haunted or not, the fact that the house had been widely reported as being haunted greatly affected its value. Nevertheless, the court dismissed the claim of fraudulent misrepresentation and said the realtor was under no duty to disclose the haunting to potential buyers.

Stambovsky promptly appealed the case and an appellate court reversed the trial court's decision to uphold the contract. The court noted that "haunting" was not a condition that a buyer or potential buyer of real property can and should be able to ascertain upon reasonable inspection of the property. In approving the action to rescind the contract, the court said: "the most meticulous inspection and the search would not reveal the presence of poltergeists at the premises or unearth the property's ghoulish reputation in the community..."

The opinion makes reference to a number of popular books and films featuring ghosts, including Shakespeare's *Hamlet* and the 1984 movie *Ghostbusters* and plays on words in a spirited manner. For example: "...in his pursuit of a legal remedy for fraudulent misrepresentation against the seller, plaintiff hasn't a ghost of a chance." And, "I am moved by the spirit of equity", and "the notion that a haunting is a condition which can and should be ascertained upon reasonable inspection of the premises is a hobgoblin which should be exorcised from the body of legal precedent."

Later that same year, Ackley sold the house to another buyer and moved to Florida. Two years later, paranormal researchers Bill Merrill and Glenn Johnson, with the aid of Helen Ackley, claimed they had contacted the ghosts in Ackley's former house, and the ghosts supposedly told them that it wasn't as much fun haunting the house without Helen. They wrote their findings in the book *Sir George: The Ghost Of Nyack*. Helen Ackley died in 2003. There have not been reports of hauntings at the house in recent years.

DEMON MURDER CASE

When Arne Johnson was charged with first-degree manslaughter of his landlord Alan Bono in 1981, the case quickly became notorious for one reason: the defense lawyer said demons possessed his client and were responsible for the murder. The case attracted international attention and became the subject of books and a made-for-television movie. It was the first time in the U.S. that demonic possession was presented as a defense.

In the year leading up to the attack on Bono, Johnson lived with his fiancée, Debbie Glatzel, whose younger brother David supposedly had been possessed by demons. During that year, the boy was the subject of several exorcisms by six priests. Johnson took part in at least one of the exorcisms and supposedly taunted the dark spirits. "Take me on, take me on instead of him," Johnson reportedly shouted.

It all began on July 3, 1980, when Debbie says David woke up sobbing, and described a vivid dream of a man with big black eyes, a thin face with animal features and jagged teeth, pointed ears, horns and hoofs. The man warned him to beware. Soon afterward, visions began to occur during the day, in the form of an old man with a white beard, wearing a flannel shirt and jeans. David also complained of invisible hands choking him and the feeling of being pummeled.

Twelve days after the first incident, the family called upon demonologists Ed and Lorraine Warren of Monroe, Connecticut to assist. They had been referred to him by their priest. Lorraine said that she saw a black, misty form next to David and that he had marks all over his body. She also claimed that he levitated, and even predicted Arne Johnson would later murder someone. In October 1980, the Warrens contacted Brookfield police to warn them that the situation was becoming dangerous.

As David's condition worsened, Debbie and Johnson moved out and found an apartment. It was then that Johnson's behavior supposedly began to change. According to Debbie, Johnson would go into a kind of trance, where he would growl, and say he saw a beast, but later he wouldn't have any memory of it. Several months later, Johnson killed his landlord during a heated argument.

Lorraine Warren called Brookfield police the day after the murder to tell them that Johnson was possessed. A "media blitz" ensued as the case attracted widespread attention. Martin Minnella, Johnson's lawyer, traveled to England to meet with lawyers who had been involved in two similar cases (though neither ever went to trial). He planned to fly in exorcism specialists from Europe and threatened to subpoena the priests involved if they would not cooperate.

The trial took place in Danbury, Connecticut Superior Court in the fall of 1981. Minnella entered the unprecedented plea of not guilty by virtue of possession by the devil. But that was as far the demon-did-it defense went. The judge barred the devil from his courtroom, saying no such defense existed.

As a result, Minnella was reduced to arguing that Johnson acted in self-defense. Johnson was convicted of first-degree manslaughter, and sentenced to 10 to 20 years in prison. He served five years, and supposedly dealt with his demons behind bars. He came out of prison a new man and married Debbie.

MORE EXORCISTS ON-CALL

The Catholic diocese of Milan, Italy started an exorcism hotline in November 2012, and doubled the number of exorcism-practicing priests from six to 12. The diocese hopes to keep up with an apparent increase in calls over the past 15 years.

"From the number of calls we receive, the need has doubled," Monsignor Angelo Mascheroni—the diocese's chief exorcist since 1995—told the news website Incrocinews. "We get young and old, men and women, people with different levels of education, from school-leavers to graduates."

Mascheroni also said that one priest was reportedly seeing as many as 120 people a day. But exorcisms are nothing new for the Catholic church. Father Gabriele Amorth, who was the Vatican's chief exorcist for 25 years, claims to have dealt with 70,000 cases of demonic possession. Father Amorth said that sex abuse scandals in the Roman Catholic Church were proof that "the Devil is at work inside the Vatican".

6

GHOST BUSTING

In the hit comedy Ghost Busters from 1984, a team of wacko para-psychologists lose their jobs at Columbia University after an encounter with a ghost. Their next move: Start a ghost exterminating service. The setup makes for some great comedic twists and turns. In reality, 'ghost busting' has a long tradition among shamans of native peoples, and today is often referred to as spirit rescue. It usually involves one or more mediums—people who attest to an ability to contact the dead.

The intent of a spirit rescue is to convince the apparition to move on to the other side, rather than cling to the earth plane. Mediums who do such work say that spirits who are intent on remaining close to the physical world do so for a variety of reasons. They might want revenge or feel possessive of someone left behind. It might relate to suicide or addiction, a fear of hell or a strong attachment to a physical place. Such ghosts supposedly have a stronger connection with people in the physical world than with spirits who are said to be ready to help them move toward the light. That's why mediums take on the role of helping such entities move on to their destination.

TAKING ACTION

Let's say you've got a ghost—something in the house that feels oppressive or just annoying. Maybe you've felt its presence, glimpsed it, noticed an unexpected smell, encountered hot or cold spots. Possibly lights flicker or a television or other electronics seemingly turn on or off by themselves. Maybe things are missing or moved around, and you're certain that no one in the house was responsible. Pets might be acting odd.

Whether or not there actually is an invisible presence in the house is irrelevant! Your actions to take control and rid the premise of the entity—imagined or real—can bring you peace of mind and maybe even help a lost soul.

Here are some guidelines for getting rid of a ghost gathered from the writings of various mediums.

—Surround yourself with a bright white light of protection. Make a strong intention that the shield will protect you, that you are safe from any invasive energy. Pretend the sun's light is so bright that it is filling you and every corner of every room.

—Identify the energy. Is it a ghost or a spirit guide? The latter are not intrusive, abusive, or frightening. You should feel uplifted if a spirit guide makes contact. A ghost probably will leave you feeling wary, fearful, upset or annoyed.

—If your ghost is a loved one who died, it could be a farewell visit. But if the ghost remains nearby, the spirit might be clinging to the earth plane. In that case, realize that it's better for both of you if the entity goes to the light.

—Research the history of the house and of the area. Did someone die in the home or area? Or was there burial ground nearby?

—Instead of thinking that ghosts are scary and dangerous, think of them as unwanted house guests. They can leave at any time. You just need to convince them to do so.

—The first thing you should do is calmly tell the ghost out loud that he or she is dead, that it's time to move on to the light. Explain that its presence is an annoyance. Sometimes they don't realize that they're dead and might even see living people as the ghosts.

—Tell the lost entity to leave. Be firm, but courteous. Reassure the ghost that there is no reason to fear moving on.

—If that doesn't work, be more forceful. But don't tell the ghost to go to hell. That might be the reason it's unwilling to move on. Demand that the entity leave immediately. Be clear and insistent, and don't harbor any regrets. Say aloud: *Leave now! Move to the light! Help is waiting for you.*

—Call on spirit guides to help, and thank them for their assistance. You might light a candle and say a prayer, calling on the spirit guides to move the lost spirit along.

—You might also try changing the energy in the house by

burning sage and carrying it around the house and through every room. Move furniture or paint the walls. More drastic measures, such as knocking out a wall, might work. But make sure that you will like the results.

If you've given your invisible intruder it's marching orders and it remains with you, it might be time to call for help from a spirit rescue group. Avoid paying for an expensive service. It's probably a psychic scam. Spirit rescue should be a free service provided by volunteers from an organization. You and your ghost are part of their continuing research, not a means of making thousands of dollars.

As one practitioner said on her web site: "The best ghost busters will calmly and firmly communicate with the energy, call in plenty of spiritual assistance and protection, and guide them to the Light."

7

TALL TALES

Ghost stories. They come in three brands: the serious, the not-so-serious, and the made up ones. There are the confirmed sightings, the stories that are hard to deny. Then there are the ones with multiple witnesses, such as ghosts at the sites of Civil War battlefields or well known haunted buildings or estates, particularly those open to visitors. Clearly, a mysterious phenomenon exists at such locales.

Every culture has folk tales about ghosts. These stories are probably a mix of fictive tales that might be based on some incident from the distant past that has been greatly expanded upon. They include the evil acts of the djinn in the Arabic world, the mysteriously alluring Encantado in Brazil, the monstrous Jikininki of Japan, and the headless horseman in America.

Finally, there are the creepy stories from the literary world—both historical and modern—ghosts who haunt the pages of novels and short stories, some by our greatest writers. That's the subject of this chapter in which some of the best known tales from the beyond—as well as some lesser known ones—are summarized through their ghostly aspects. We start near the turn of the 17th century and work our way forward in time.

HAMLET, WILLIAM SHAKESPEARE

We have to start with William Shakespeare. While he was hardly a horror writer, he definitely had an interest in the supernatural—especially ghosts.

Hamlet's recently deceased father is by far the creepiest among them, sneaking up on *Hamlet* with blood trickling from his ear, demanding revenge. Hamlet was published in 1603, and probably written between 1599-1601. Some critics have suggested that Hamlet is imagining the ghost, that the ghost sounds a lot like Hamlet himself. After all, he says to Horatio: "My father! —me thinks I see my father...in my mind's eye."

But Horatio sees him, too, and so do the castle guards. Horatio tells Hamlet that the guards Marcellus and Bernado saw:

"A figure like your father,
Armed at point exactly, cap-a-pe,
Appears before them, and with solemn march
Goes slowly and stately by them."

And later Hamlet becomes much more assertive about the issue:

"It is a damned ghost that we have seen."

So it seems the critics should give the bard a break. Shakespeare is writing about real ghosts, not imaginary ones.

THE CASTLE OF OTRANTO, HORACE WALPOLE

Published in 1764, *The Castle of Otranto* by Horace Walpole is considered the first gothic novel, a genre that would become wildly popular in the later 18th century and early 19th century, forbearers of well-known gothic tales, such as Dracula and Frankenstein.

However, when Walpole wrote the novel he used a pseudonym and described it as a translation of an Italian manuscript printed in Naples in 1529 that had been rediscovered in the library of "an ancient Catholic family in the north of England." The Italian manuscript's story, it was claimed, was derived from a story dating back as to the Crusades. However, it was all fiction. The so-called Italian manuscript, along with its alleged author, Onuphrio Muralto, were Walpole's fictional creations, and William Marshal was his pseudonym.

The story involves ghostly activities in a castle occupied by an overbearing lord and his family. Out of nowhere a huge supernatural helmet falls on the lord's son, crushing him to death on his wedding day. That triggers concern over a prophecy that the family, without an heir, would lose the castle. Walpole's haunted castle tale introduces many elements of future gothic novels, such as mysterious sounds, doors opening on their own, and a beautiful heroine fleeing from a depraved male figure.

THE MASQUE OF THE RED DEATH, EDGAR ALLAN POE

Poe is at his gruesome best in this short story, published in 1845. A horrific disease runs rampant in the countryside, causing its victims to die quickly and gruesomely. But behind the locked gates of his palace Prince Prospero remains content and unconcerned. To celebrate his wealth and well-being, he throws a fancy masquerade ball. That's the setup for a tale about a ghost that disrupts the prince's masked ball.

In planning the celebration, Prospero decorates the rooms of his house in different colors. The easternmost room is decorated in blue, the next one in purple. The rooms continue westward, in the following color scheme: green, orange, white, and violet. The seventh room is black, with red windows. An ebony clock stands in this room, and when the clock rings loudly each hour, everyone grows quiet and uneasy, and the orchestra stops playing.

The rooms are so beautiful and strange that the revelers are entranced as they move from one to the next. Most guests, however, avoid the final, black-and-red room because it contains both the clock and an ominous ambience.

At midnight, a new guest appears, ghoulishly masqueraded as a victim of the Red Death. His mask looks like the face of death, his clothing resembles a funeral shroud, and he heads right for the black-and-red room with an outraged Prospero trailing after him.

A CHRISTMAS CAROL, CHARLES DICKENS

The dead are what move Ebenezer Scrooge out of his bitter, miserly ways. Marley's ghost, and the ghosts of Christmas past, present, and yet to come ultimately transform the penurious businessman, whose name has become synonymous with penny-pinching and lack of generosity. Probably the most influential ghost story ever written, Charles Dickens's famed novella, published in 1843, served to resurrect the spirit of Christmas and led to a new practice of sending Christmas cards and decorating Christmas trees.

THE TURN OF THE SCREW, HENRY JAMES

Published in 1898, James' novel is about a governess on an estate who sees the ghosts of her predecessor and another deceased member of the staff. The two children in her care appear under the spell of the ghosts and seemingly are aware of their existence on the property. The paranormal influence on the children causes one to flee, and the other to die in the arms of the governess, the ghost hovering nearby.

In spite of that scenario, many literary critics suggest that the ghosts were all in the mind of the governess. In other words, it was a story of psychological horror, minus real ghosts. The implication is that stories of imaginary ghosts are better stories than tales where the fictive ghosts are 'real.' The ghost-busting critics seem to be telling us that ghosts are not real in the everyday world, so they shouldn't be real in literary fiction, either.

The problem with attaching that point of view onto *The Turn of the Screw* is that in his notes and letters about the story, Henry James himself never indicated that the ghosts weren't real. In all likelihood, James wrote a straightforward Gothic tale. Ghosts and all.

THE HAUNTING ON HOUSE HILL, SHIRLEY JACKSON

This creepy 1959 ghost story by Shirley Jackson was a finalist for the National Book Award and is considered one of the best literary ghost tales of the twentieth century. The *Wall Street Journal* called it the best haunted house story ever written. Contributing to the eeriness of the tale is the interplay between the evil consciousness of the 80-year-old mansion and the emotions and psychological makeup of the four people who come there to investigate the supernatural happenings.

Dr. John Montague, a paranormal investigator, hopes to find scientific evidence of the existence of ghosts. He rents Hill House for the summer and invites several people chosen because of their past experience with paranormal events. Only two accept: Eleanor Vance, a shy, reclusive young woman and Theodora, a flamboyant bohemian artist. The fourth person staying at the house is Luke Sanderson, the young heir to Hill House.

All four experience strange events, including sounds and unseen spirits roaming the halls at night, strange writing on the walls and other unexplained phenomena. Eleanor seems to attract the most attention from the house and her presence may even generate some of the phenomenon.

THE OTHER, THOMAS TRYON

Niles and Holland Perry are 13-year-old twins residing in a small Connecticut town. The boys are close, but different. Niles is kind and helpful; Holland is brash and troublesome. The extended family has gathered to mourn the death of the twins' father. Their mother hasn't recovered from the gruesome accidental death, and the boys roam free on summer break.

Holland's behavior turns darker and Niles can no longer ignore his cruel tricks. The story has one of the most shocking twists in modern fiction.

THE SHINING, STEPHEN KING

Old Mr. Halloran recognized that five-year-old Danny was a 'shiner,' a psychic powerhouse. When Danny's father became caretaker of the Overlook Hotel, the boy's visions expand as he awakens spirits from the past. The success of *The Shining*, published in 1977, established King as the preeminent author in the horror genre.

As winter storms close in, cutting off the caretakers from the rest of the world, the hotel literally develops a life of its own as masked guests ride the elevator and the ghostly bartenders serve the partying crowd of spirits. At the heart of the ghostly activities is an evil force that invades the minds of the caretaker and his family.

GHOST STORY, PETER STRAUB

Considered a gothic classic, the 1979 novel offers all the nuances of the genre—creepy atmospherics, mood shifts and character nuances. An incident from decades ago comes back to haunt four aging men in the town of Milburn, New York, who thought they could get away with murder. Now vengeful entities are out to destroy the town as they conjure dark fears and nightmares.

ESPERANZA, TRISH J MACGREGOR

Finally, a novel from 2010 that I cannot ignore, written by my wife. Imagine an ancient cult of hungry ghosts who possess humans, using their bodies for passion and terror. *Esperanza* is the first of a trilogy of hungry ghost tales, followed by *Ghost Key* and *Apparition*.

Tess Livingston met Ian Ritter at a roadside stop high in the Ecuadorian Andes, waiting for a bus to the mysterious town of

Esperanza. Tess is an FBI agent who remembers tracking a group of international counterfeiters. But she doesn't remember booking a trip to Esperanza. Ian is a journalist who was planning to vacation in the Galapagos Islands. He, too, isn't quite sure why he has a ticket to Esperanza. Their meeting will change their lives forever as they discover that they hold the key in a mystical war between spirits of the dead who guard humanity and the hungry ghosts who exist to possess and destroy.

8

BEHIND THE SCENES

Considering the subject matter, it's somehow not surprising that uncanny incidents occurred behind the scenes of some of the scariest supernatural movies ever made. The real-life horrors took place during the filming, and after it was over. Among the movies subjected to such incidents are *The Exorcist, The Omen, Poltergeist, The Crow.*

THE EXORCIST

Voted the scariest horror movie of all time by Entertainment Weekly and Maxim, the *Exorcist* graphically portrays an epic struggle between human lives and demonic forces. The film debuted in 1973 as an adaptation of William Peter Blatty's best-selling novel that became a occult classic, an icon of popular culture.

Peculiar events plagued the cast and crew throughout the production of the movie, including the death of two cast members. At least six people associated with The Exorcist died either during production or prior to the release of the movie. Actor Jack McGowan died of flu complications a little over a month before the movie's release. McGowan portrayed Burke Dennings, the life of the party, who tells a prominent senator, "There seems to be an alien pubic hair in my gin." Dennings also dies in the movie at the hands of the possessed Regan.

Vasiliki Maliaros was 90 years old when she died of natural causes not long after she finished filming her role as Father Karras' mother. During production of the film, a night watchman for the set and the set refrigeration technician also passed away.

Linda Blair, who played Regan, lost her grandfather during the filming. Max Von Sydow, who played Father Merrin, was in good health at the beginning of production, but suffered from a series of unexplained illnesses during the shoot. His brother died during the filming.

On several occasions, lights that had been rigged to the ceilings of sets fell without explanation, fortunately never hurting anybody. Delays were also caused when props were regularly shipped or delivered to incorrect locations or simply disappeared from sets.

The film took a major blow when an unexplained fire destroyed all of the interior sets of the MacNeill residence, except Regan's bedroom! That delayed filming six weeks for the last scenes in Iraq in which a small statue of the demon, Pazuzu, would be discovered.

Ellen Burstyn accepted the role of Regan's mom only after producers agreed to eliminate her character's scripted line, "I believe in the devil!" She might've thought that some sort of demons were at work on the set when she was injured filming the scene in which Regan throws her across the bedroom with superhuman strength. In reality, Ellen Burstyn was yanked by a harness, but she landed on her coccyx, resulting in a permanent spinal injury.

Astonishingly, snow fell on the indoor set of the demon-inhabited bedroom. Although it was explainable, it was startling. In order to provide the effect of visible breath, the set was refrigerated and cooled by four air conditioners. Temperatures often plunged below freezing and on one occasion when the air was saturated with moisture, the cast and crew arrived to find a layer of snow covering the set.

In the scene where Father Karras discovers that Regan's demon is speaking English in reverse, a white banner is visible above a door that reads: "TASUKETE" in stark red letters. Translated from Japanese, it shouts: "HELP!" The banner was part of an unrelated project in Keating Hall on Fordham University's Bronx campus where the scene was filmed.

THE STORY BEHIND THE EXORCIST

William Peter Blatty based his best-selling novel on a newspaper story he read as a 20-year-old English literature major at Georgetown University. The article by Billy Brinkley appeared in the August 20, 1949 issue of the Washington Post and was headlined, "Priest Frees

Mt. Rainier Boy Reported Held In Devil's Grip." It told the story of a 14-year-old boy from Mount Rainier, Maryland who supposedly was possessed and how a Catholic priest freed the boy by performing the ancient ritual of exorcism. (It was latter learned that the boy was actually 13 years old and from Cottage City, Maryland.)

For years the notion of demonic possession stuck in Blatty's mind, and twenty years later, he began writing *The Exorcist*. He finished the novel during the summer of 1971. As part of his research, Blatty contacted the priest who had conducted the actual exorcism. The letter Blatty received revealed that a diary was kept by an attending priest, who recorded daily events related to the ongoing exorcism.

Blatty requested to see the diary, but the priest refused. After Blatty changed the lead character from a 14-year-old boy to a 12-year-old girl, he obtained a copy of the diary and based much of his book and movie on the material. The diary revealed that the exorcism was partially performed in both Cottage City, Maryland and Belnor, Missouri. Several area newspapers at the time reported on a speech a minister gave to an amateur parapsychology society in which he claimed to have exorcised a demon from the boy named Robbie, and that the ordeal lasted a little more than six weeks.

A film called *The Haunted Boy—The Secret Diary of the Exorcist* was released in 2012. It was based to an article *Haunted Boy*, by Mark Opsasnick that appeared in *Strange* Magazine.

POLTERGEIST

Like *The Exorcist*, the legendary *Poltergeist* movies are a part of popular culture—at least the creepy side of it. The simple phrase: "The-e-e-y're here," instantly reminds us of the chilling scene in which the little girl, Carol Anne Freeling, is abducted by evil spirits in the TV.

In the pool scene, the skeletons that emerge from the muddy water were real. JoBeth Williams was unaware of this until the scene had already been filmed. Director William Friedkin felt somewhat uneasy about the matter and possibly sensing what was coming, asked technical advisor Reverend Thomas Bermingham to exorcise the set. He gave a blessing and talked to the cast and crew to reassure them, but refused to perform an exorcism, saying it might increase anxiety.

The presence of real skeletons on the set might've been a premonition of strange events related to the movie, including the death of two young actresses who played sisters.

Julian Beck who played the bad spirit' in *Poltergeist II*, died of stomach cancer in 1985. Two years later, Will Sampson who played the 'good spirit' in Poltergeist II, died after receiving a heart-lung transplant. Will was also known as the tall 'mute' Indian in *One Flew Over The Cuckoo's Nest*.

While the two men had medical conditions, more strange were the death of the two girls. Dominique Dunn, who played the older sister in the first Poltergeist movie, was strangled by her ex-lover shortly after the release of the first movie in 1982. Six years later, Heather O'Rourke, who played the little girl Carol Anne in all three movies, died of congenital intestinal stenosis at the age of 12. She was on a break from filming *Poltergeist III* at the time and a replacement was used in parts of the film. Ironically, Dominique Dunn and Heather O'Rourke, the on-screen sisters, are buried in the same cemetery.

THE OMEN

A classic horror film about the devil's offspring, *The Omen* might be the most cursed film of the genre. Before and during the filming, there were many...omens. A series of peculiar accidents plagued the cast, crew and even people loosely connected to the film. The strange occurrences began with a series of unlikely lightning strikes.

Before filming began, the plane carrying novelist and screenwriter David Seltzer was struck by lightning, and he was lucky to survive. In another electrifying incident, a plane transporting the films star Gregory Peck was also struck by lightning. The pilot managed to land the plane safely and nobody was hurt. During filming in Rome, a bolt of lightning narrowly missed producer Harvey Bernhard.

Peck had another close brush with death during the filming, when he cancelled a flight to Israel that crashed and killing all onboard. With all the strange happenings, it was a wonder that Peck decided to continue on with the project. Similarly, it's surprising that director Richard Donner didn't walk away from *The Omen* when he was hit by a car, and stayed at a hotel that was bombed by the IRA. In a separate vehicle related incident, a number of crew members were nearly killed on the first day of shooting in a head-on car crash.

As another omen, the poster for the movie depicted the silhouette of a boy with a wolf-like shadow. The movie title was above the image and below it were the words: YOU HAVE BEEN WARNED.

THE CROW

Tragedy and irony, as well as mystery and intrigue, overtook the plot maneuvers of this comic book adaptation when real life and fiction collided head-on in the making of this cult classic. The film's star, Brandon Lee, was accidentally shot and killed with a life bullet in a scene in which he was to be murdered, and his death led to rumors of an actual murder.

Like *The Omen*, the production was cursed from day one of shooting, Feb. 1, 1993, when a carpenter was badly shocked and burned after a lift he was operating struck high-voltage power cables. Other incidents included a grip truck catching fire, a stuntman falling through the roof of one of the sets, a handyman crashing his car through the studio's plaster shop, and a member of the crew accidentally stabbing a screwdriver through his hand. Six weeks into the shoot, a powerful storm destroyed a number of elaborate set pieces that delayed the shooting schedule.

Somehow, the production finally wrapped. As a result of the tragedy and mystery surrounding the making of *The Crow*, the film stood out from the plethora of horror films and led to its cult status.

PART TWO
SPIRIT GUIDES

9

GUIDING REFLECTIONS

If you think of ghosts as minor league players in the spirit world, then spirit guides are on the all-star team. While ghosts might be feared or dreaded, or just a spooky annoyance, spirit guides are more benevolent, helpful and inspiring. Throughout history they have been welcomed and called upon for their guiding light. Their primary message, it seems, is that there is no death, only transformation from the physical to other states of being.

Deceased friends or relatives might serve as your spirit guides, contacting you through dreams or visions. Whether you think that contact is real or imagined, or you're not certain, is immaterial if the information you receive is helpful.

Sonia Choquette, author and intuitive counselor, refers to spirit guides as assistants. "They're there to help you in practical areas; they're your helpers. They might help you in health matters; those are healers. They might be there to help you evolve your consciousness; those are teachers. They might just be there just to help lighten your heavy emotional life; those are joy guides. And they're all there to help your journey on earth be a more positive, successful, and pleasurable one."

People of all cultures, from the times, have interacted with spirit guides. Let's take a brief look at some of the highlights of spirit contact over the ages, starting with the ancient Greeks. While people have always looked to the dead, particularly ancestors, for guidance, and done so through a variety of means, one particular method stands out. It's called mirror-gazing and in ancient times often involved a psychomanteum, a dimly lit isolated room with a mirror or reflective surface, such as a pool of water.

ORACLE OF THE DEAD

You've probably heard about the famed Oracle of Delphi, where ancient Greeks journeyed to hear prophecies from a priestess serving as the oracle. Lesser known is the Oracle of the Dead, a site in northwest Greece that pilgrims visited to contact the dead and learn of their future.

The Oracle of the Dead, built in the third century BC, included a complex of underground passageways and isolation cells. It was the ancient Greek's premier psychomanteum, and was also known as The Necromanteion of Ephyra. Placed in the cells, pilgrims fasted and underwent sensory deprivation, exhaustion and disorientation—all designed to create an environment to induce visions. They also wandered about dark passageways and a stone labyrinth.

After several days, and sometimes weeks, the pilgrims were ready to meet the souls of the dead. They descended to the Sacred Hall in an underground cavern where they were given hallucinogenic leaves or seeds to chew. The pilgrims then gazed into a large copper cauldron filled with water where they saw visions of the dead in the dark, reflective surface. In their heightened state, it was said that dead friends and relatives sometimes emerged from the reflective cauldron and appeared as if they were physical beings.

Very little was known about the Greek psychomanteums until 1958 when archaeologist Sotirios Dakaris and his team uncovered a series of small underground rooms connected by a passageway that led to the main chamber where they found the remains of a large copper cauldron ringed with a banister. They had discovered the Oracle of the Dead, spoken of by Homer and Herodotus.

THE AZTEC MIRROR

In the 16th century, John Dee, a famed English mathematician, astronomer and astrologer used an Aztec mirror to make contact with the dead. Dee studied alchemy and divination while straddling the worlds of science and magic, and made extensive use of his mirror while pursuing his occult interests. He was also the officer scryer or crystal gazer for Queen Elizabeth I.

Made of highly-polished obsidian, the black mirror was brought to Europe after the conquest of Mexico by Cortés between 1527 and

1530. Black mirrors in Mexico were associated with Tezcatlipoca, the dark god of war and sorcery, whose name can be translated as 'Smoking Mirror.' Aztec priests used mirrors for divination and conjuring visions.

No doubt Dee was knowledgeable about the Greek's use of psychomanteum, or mirror-gazing and that added to his fascination with the Aztec mirror.

RAYMOND MOODY'S PSYCHOMANTEUM

Years after psychiatrist Raymond Moody wrote Life After Life, the classic book on near-death experiences, he wanted to find a way that anyone could connect with the afterlife without having to die briefly and be revived.

A scholar of ancient Greece, Moody eventually found his answer when he read the Greek magical papyri—scrolls of magical recipes found in Egypt, but written in Greek. "By following the instruction of the magical papyri in a facility designed for just this purpose, I had created a modern psychomanteum in the style of the ancient Greeks," he wrote in his autobiography *Paranormal*.

He named his psychomanteum the John Dee Theater of the Mind, and began looking for people willing to step into his 'apparition booth.' His goal was to answer the question: Can apparitions of deceased loved ones make themselves known in a controlled environment to normal, healthy people?

In preparation, he would spend hours with his patients discussing the loved one they wanted to encounter. Then he would escort the person into his mirror-gazing booth and turn on a light that was about as bright as a single candle. He would tell the patient to relax, gaze deeply into the mirror, and think only of the one he wanted to see. They would remain in the booth for as long as they liked and Moody would discuss their experience with him afterwards.

Moody was surprised that five of his first ten subjects saw and communicated with an apparition, and all five believed that they had actually connected with a deceased loved on. He had expected one or two contacts and doubts about the reality of the contact.

His first subject, a 44-year-old nurse whose husband had died two years earlier, made contact, but not in the way that she or Moody had expected. They had talked for hours about her late husband. But when she emerged from the booth, she had a puzzled expression. She had made contact, but with her father, not her husband. She was stunned by the experience, because he had actually come out of the mirror to talk to her.

In all, Moody led 300 subjects into the psychomanteum for his mirror-gazing experiment that he wrote about in his book, *Reunions*. He viewed the room as a therapeutic tool to heal grief and bring insight.

JUNG'S TOWER

For renowned psychotherapist Carl Jung, contact with spirit guides seemed linked to a tower he built on the shore of Lake Zurich. Although he didn't gaze at mirrors, his tower inadvertently served a psychomanteum. Beginning in 1924, Jung spent long periods of time alone in the tower.

He wrote about how living in the tower allowed him to develop his inner life:

"At Bollingen I am in the midst of my true life, I am most deeply myself….At times I feel as if I am spread out over the landscape and inside things, and am myself living in every tree, in the splashing of the waves, in the clouds and the animals that come and go, in the procession of the seasons….I pump the water from the well. I chop the wood and cook the food. These simple acts make man simple; and how difficult it is to be simple!"

His exploration of archetypes and the collective unconscious during his isolation in the tower seemed to attract experiences from invisible realms. "He heard music, as if an orchestra were playing; he glimpsed a host of young peasant men who seemed to be encircling the tower with much laughter, singing, and roughhousing," wrote *Deirdre Bair in Jung: A Biography.*

10

VICTORIAN REVIVAL

The belief that we survive death and that the living can communicate with the deceased dates back to primitive times, but by the 19th century prevalent religious, scientific, and cultural forces ridiculed and dismissed any claims of contact with realms beyond the physical world.

So it was a surprise when contact with the spirit world suddenly flourished in the second half of that century and into the early twentieth century. The belief that it's possible to commune with the dead became the basis of a religion, spiritualism, and communities developed around the religion.

Historians point to one event that triggered the renewed interest in contact with the dead. It took place in a hamlet that no longer exists and involved three sisters, who became famous or infamous, depending on your perspective.

The Fox family moved into a cottage in Hydesville, New York, after the previous tenants had left because of strange noises coming from the walls. Soon the Foxes were also plagued by a mysterious rapping. One night, John Fox was determined to find its source. He rattled the windows, expecting to find loose sashes. After he stopped, he heard a similar rattle, as if in reply. When his 12-year-old daughter Kate clapped her hands, the same number of taps responded as if invisible knuckles rapped against the wall.

Eventually, the Fox sisters created a code with the invisible rapper and were told by the entity that he was a murdered peddler named Charles B. Rosna, whose body was buried beneath the cabin. Astonishingly, fifty-six years later, investigators actually dug up a skeleton in the cellar.

News of the mysterious rappings became the talk of the small town and soon attracted widespread attention as interest in contacting the dead became a popular pastime. The rappings not only disrupted the Fox family, but ultimately instigated a new metaphysical movement. March 31, 1848, the day communication began, is now considered the birthday of spiritualism. Throngs of people on both sides of the Atlantic attempted to make contact with departed family members and friends and spirit guides. By 1855, two million people were followers of the movement.

Four decades later, Maggie Fox who was in dire financial straits, claimed the sisters had faked the rapping. She was paid to make the public announcement in front of an audience. Her explanation was that the sisters could crack their toes to make the rapping sound.

That didn't explain the body that would be dug up below the house, or the intensity of the rapping. According to William Crookes, a prominent British scientist, who examined Kate Fox between 1871 and 1874, the sound was "loud enough to hear several rooms off." He became convinced the rapping phenomenon was not faked. However, a year later Maggie retracted the confession.

However, once a few con artists were exposed, many critics of spiritualism proclaimed all mediums were frauds. By the turn of the 20th century, the heyday of spiritualism was coming to an end as enthusiasm for contacting the spirit world faded. Ardent skeptics attacked the movement with a vengeance, as did religious leaders, who instilled fear of the devil into their congregations.

Today, there are about 150 spiritualist churches in the U.S. The best known centers of spiritualism are the Cassadaga Lake Free Association in Lily Dale, New York, and the Cassadaga Spiritualist Camp in central Florida.

ARTHUR CONAN DOYLE

During the years when spiritualism was under heavy attack, one surprising supporter stepped forward to defend the movement and to confirm what spiritualists believed about contact with the dead was true. Sir Arthur Conan Doyle, creator of the renowned super-rational detective Sherlock Holmes, believed it was possible to contact spirits of the dead.

When the British author, who called himself an agnostic as

an adult, experienced contact with the dead through mediums, he remained open-minded and refused to call it impossible. His interest in spiritualism grew out of the death of his first-born son, who died in World War I. It became a life-long obsession even though it damaged his reputation.

He and illusionist Harry Houdini became friends and shared an interest in spiritualism. But they clashed when Houdini began exposing fake mediums and claimed that all 'spiritualist tricks' could be replicated by magicians.

HOUDINI

Harry Houdini wanted to believe that communication with spirits was possible. The loss of his mother devastated him, and he tried repeatedly to contact her through mediums. But as a skilled magician and illusionist, he soon recognized fellow magicians involved in the act, and turned to exposing such fake mediums. Thereafter, he became known as an ardent skeptic and debunker.

Yet, his death revealed that he had never completely dispelled his interest in spiritualism. In spite of his debunking efforts, he pledged to his wife that upon his death he would try to contact her through a secret code.

Houdini died on Halloween, October 31, 1926 of peritonitis— internal poisoning resulting from a ruptured appendix. At the time of his death, he was planning an endurance stunt that would require him to survive entombment in a coffin. To create excitement for the upcoming stunt, Houdini exhibited the coffin in the lobby of his theater shows. Ironically, that coffin was used to transport his body back to New York City for burial.

For the next ten years on October 31, his wife Bess held séances and waited to hear the secret code, proving that life after death existed. These séances were always attended by prominent magicians, as well as some of Houdini's friends.

In early 1929, Bess Houdini was approached by a young medium named Arthur Ford, who began working at breaking the code. During the sessions Ford supposedly would fall asleep and his spirit guide Fletcher would speak through him while communicating with Houdini. After several séances over a ten-week period, he presented the code to Bess. She signed a witnessed statement verifying that

Ford had broken the code. But it wasn't long before debunkers attacked Ford and Bess charging, among other things, that Bess had revealed the code to newspaper reporters a year earlier.

The code was a phrase that Houdini and Bess had used years before in their vaudeville mind-reading act. The message was, "Rosabelle- answer- tell-pray, answer- look- tell- answer, answer- tell."

Ford's spirit guide Fletcher relayed one final message from Houdini.

"He says, 'Tell the whole world that Harry Houdini still lives and will prove it a thousand times and more.' He is pretty excited. He says, 'I was perfectly honest and sincere in trying to disprove survival, though I resorted to tricks to prove my point for the simple reason that I did not believe communication was true, but I did no more than seemed justifiable. I am now sincere in sending this through in my desire to undo. Tell all those who lost faith because of my mistake to lay hold again of hope, and to live with the knowledge that life is continuous. That is my message to the world, through my wife and through this instrument.'"

11

MEDIUM CENTRAL

The quaint town of Cassadaga is nestled in a hilly pine forest in Central Florida, a few miles from Interstate 4, which connects the rural town with bustling Orlando half an hour away. Established in 1894, it's the most unusual town in Florida, a community where nearly every resident is a medium who specializes in contact with spirits. Outside the border of the Cassadaga Spiritualist Camp, as it is known, reside other mediums and psychics attracted to the mystical energy of this hamlet, which looks and feels like a place from another era.

The town includes a 90-year old Mediterranean-style hotel, an auditorium, a café, post office and several New Age shops offering books, crystals and other esoteric paraphernalia, and psychic readings. On weekends, the small town fills with enough tourists to wake the dead—so to speak—and the two-story Cassadaga Hotel is often fully booked. The rooms are modest and slightly spooky in their own right. Visitors won't find a television in the room, but there may be a ghost prowling the hallways at night.

Visitors meander along the old, narrow streets passing 1920s-style wood-framed houses with front porches. Many of the houses feature hanging placards offering their services, and the mediums are referred to as reverends.

Spirit Lake and Colby Lake border an expansive park with hiking trails just outside the residential streets and not far from Colby Temple, where spiritualist services are held. On one Sunday in September 2012, more than a hundred people were in attendance at a service. Most were local residents and members of the spiritualist church. A handful of visitors were also in attendance, including a few who had joined an orb photography tour the night before.

For those unfamiliar with tenets of spiritualism, a pamphlet explained that spiritualism's main focus is to "promote an individual's personal experience with God," adding that "Any attempt to personalize the idea of God only limits the totality of that Intelligence, which is the reason that Spiritualists sometimes refer to that idea of God as *Infinite Intelligence or Infinite Spirit*." According to the philosophy of spiritualism, "all religions can produce enlightenment, and believes that Jesus, as well as all other saviors and prophets, was a real person."

The pamphlet goes on to say that spiritualism includes the belief of survival of the personality after death, and that such survival can be proved through mediumship. "Belief in the survival of the personality also removes grieving when it is realized that our loved ones are still around us from time to time, are able to communicate with us…from the spirit realm."

The spiritualist service that day began with the deceptive flavor of a Southern Baptist service with the singing of several old gospel songs from a hymnal led by a woman playing an organ. After a couple of songs and announcements, another woman, a spiritualist reverend who was acting as moderator, called for all the healers at the service to assemble at the back of the room. Nine men and women took their places behind empty chairs, then those who wanted a healing were told to line up along the side wall and wait their turn.

While the healers were working, holding their hands several inches from the heads of those in the healing seats, the reverend led the rest of those assembled into a relaxed, meditative state with a guided visualization that focused on a serene, bucolic setting. No fire-and-brimstone here; no male figure leading the congregation, and instead of a life-sized crucifix, the backdrop on the stage was a pair of large painting of sunflowers.

As the healers finished, the moderator introduced a guest lecturer, another female spiritualist reverend, a medium who resides in Cassadaga. She gave a humorous talk that emphasized positive thinking and finding joy in everyday life. After another song, she returned to the pulpit and began what makes the spiritualist way unique among church services. Instead of giving communion or reading bible verses, she offered spot readings to people in the audience, each one lasting a few minutes. She talked about relationships, health issues, travel and other changes taking place in each person's life. It was difficult to judge how accurate they were, but there was no shortage of raised hands when she finished with one reading and moved to the next.

THE MEDIUM AND THE SPIRIT GUIDE

The roots of Cassadaga go back to 1874 when, during a late summer séance in Lake Mills, Iowa, George Colby, a 27-year old medium from Pike, New York, received a message from an Indian spirit named Seneca. In some accounts, Colby reportedly said that Seneca manifested in physical form and instructed him to immediately leave Iowa and make contact with T. D. Giddings, a medium in Eau Claire, Wisconsin.

The two men, according to Colby's account, were to conduct another séance through which Seneca would spiritually commune with them. When they did so, they entered a trance-like state and were told that, "A congress of spirits had selected Florida for the establishment of a great spiritualist center, and that Colby had been chosen to lead in its creation."

In a series of spiritual sessions that followed, Colby continued receiving directions from his spirit guide, Seneca. He was told that the proposed location of this new spiritual center would be "... near Blue Springs, Florida, on high pine hills overlooking a chain of silvery lakes." It wasn't long before Colby and the entire Giddings family headed for Florida.

They boarded a steamboat in Jacksonville and, on the night of November 1, 1875, landed at Blue Springs, then a remote settlement of a couple of clapboard structures on the St. Johns River. Because of limited accommodations at Blue Springs, the Colby party resided temporarily in palmetto hut to await further instructions from Seneca. Then, late one night in the faint light of a kerosene lamp, they were contacted by Seneca with orders to "Go east, to the outskirts of the village and find the seven hills, this will be the place."

The next morning, traveling by mule and wagon, they headed from Blue Springs along a rutted sandy road that cut eastward through palmettos and slash pines. Near the town of present day

Lake Helen, they found seven pine-covered hills, and saw the silvery lakes mentioned by Seneca. Both Colby and Giddings agreed that this was the spot where they were to build a new spiritual center.

For many years, the Colby and Giddings' homesteads were frequented by mediums from the Cassadaga Free Lakes Association, of Cassadaga, New York, where they had attended summer spiritualist camp meetings. But it wasn't until October of 1894 that a group of these mediums established the charter for the Southern Cassadaga Spiritualist Camp Meeting Association on 35 acres, and the camp later expanded to 57 acres.

By 1895, Cassadaga was becoming a winter retreat for spiritualists. In the early 1900s, advertisements in northern newspapers invited mediums to permanently relocate to the growing spiritualist camp. By the 1920s, Cassadaga had become a regular settlement and a center of spiritualism. In 1922, the historic Cassadaga Hotel was built to accommodate the increasing number of visitors and mediums. George Colby died on July 27, 1933, his spirit-guided vision of a new center for Spiritualism a reality.

The first spiritual meetings attracted many local residents, but since they were unfamiliar with spiritualism, Cassadaga was soon looked upon as a strange place, "where the devil's work is done...where they talk to spooks." Backwoods preachers warned their congregations to "stay away from Cassadaga, less ye be damned." Even today, ministers in some neighboring towns warn their congregations not to be enticed into the wayward ways of Cassadaga.

PRINCIPALS OF SPIRITUALISM

We believe in Infinite Intelligence.

We believe that the phenomena of nature, both physical and spiritual, are the expression of Infinite Intelligence.

We affirm that a correct understanding of such expression and living in accordance therewith constitute true religion.

We affirm that the existence and personal identity of the individual continue after the change called death.

We affirm that communication with the so-called dead is a fact, scientifically proven by the phenomena of Spiritualism.

We believe that the highest morality is contained in the Golden

Rule: "Whatsoever ye would that others should do unto you, do ye also unto them."

We affirm the moral responsibility of the individual, and that he makes his own happiness or unhappiness as he obeys or disobeys Nature's physical and spiritual laws.

We affirm that the doorway to reformation is never closed against any human soul, here or hereafter.

We affirm that the Precepts of Prophecy and Healing contained in the Bible are Divine attributes proven through Mediumship.

HAUNTED HOTEL

While the Cassadaga Hotel fills up on weekends, one chilly weekday night in the winter of 1992, Trish and I and our young daughter were the sole occupants of the hotel. We had our choice of rooms and selected one on the second floor. We walked around the town that afternoon, pushing Megan along in her stroller. Trish had a reading with one of the camp mediums, Hazel Burley.

Hazel has resided in Cassadaga since 1970, longer than any other medium. Years later, on a return trip to Cassadaga, I would have a reading I would consider remarkable because of one comment. She told me that she was getting a message from someone with the letter 'J,' who had died with a brain-related disorder. She paused, then said, "No, there are two of them." She was right. A friend and a cousin both had died within the past year, both of brain cancer. One's name was Jay, the other was John. Was she in contact with one or both of them or did she pick up the information psychically? Either way, I was impressed.

As we entered the hotel that evening in 1992 after eating dinner in nearby Lake Helen, I was struck by how eerily quiet it was. The stairs and the old wooden floor creaked and groaned as we made our way to our room. We settled in for the evening with our books. We didn't bother locking the doors. The town was deserted, the hotel empty, what was the point?

Around eleven or twelve, we turned off the lights. Megan had fallen asleep earlier. Just as we were drifting off, we heard a thunderous stomp of feet coming from the other end of the hallway. I sat up, listening. It sounded like someone wearing heavy boots who intentionally pounded the floor.

I got up, turned on the light, and moved to the door to take a look. The thudding sound came closer and closer. It was so loud and powerful it felt as if the entire hotel was shaking. I placed my hand on the doorknob just as the stomping stopped in front of our door. A chill swept through me accompanied by a feeling of intense dread. A sense of profound malevolence electrified the air; that's the only way I can describe it. I was certain that if I opened the door, whoever, whatever stood on the other side would force its way into the room. I slid the bolt over, locking the door.

Trish was right behind me, and feeling the same way. Without exchanging a word, we both shoved the heavy wooden dresser in front of the door. We stood there terrified that whatever it was would break through our defenses. The door knob turned, rattled. Or was it our imagination? The inside of my mouth flashed desert dry. We simultaneously reached for Megan, scooping her off the other bed. I don't know where we thought we would escape if whatever was on the other side of that door broke in. There was no fire escape, just a roof—and a long jump to the ground.

I held up my hand, whispered, "Listen!"

We held our breaths. Something had changed, a pressure released. I no longer felt the presence. The hallway was silent. "It's gone," I said.

After a few minutes, we went back to bed, but we kept the dresser in front of the door. It seemed silly in retrospect. Couldn't a ghost walk through a door? Maybe not without an invitation.

In the morning, we mentioned the disturbance to the night clerk who was still on duty. Astonishingly, he said he heard nothing. "The ghosts are friendly here," he said, somewhat defensively.

12

NATURE SPIRITS

Elves, sprites, fairies—spirits of flowers, woods, and the country-side. Those are the best known nature spirits, who work in coordination with devas and elementals. Add to that list the apu, spirits of the mountains, especially in the Andes, the former realm of the Incas.

The nature spirits and their allies are said to have been here since the beginning of time, before the arrival of mankind. They are responsible for developing the physical landscape of the natural world. In traditional cultures, especially those that worshipped the Goddess as Mother Nature, tribal members made offerings to these deities whom they considered divine beings in control of particular natural phenomena. In the Western World, nature spirits are largely considered mythological beings personifying aspects of nature.

In shamanic traditions, these beings now live in the Middle World—an alternate or parallel Earth. In an article entitled *Shamanism: Healing of Individuals and the Planet,* Sandra Ingerman, a shamanic teacher, writes:

"The Middle World is one place where the shaman can speak to the spirit of the rocks, trees, plants, wind, water, fire, earth, etc. The shaman can speak to the spirit that lives in all things here. The Middle World is also inhabited by a variety of spirits such as 'the hidden folk.' The hidden folk are the fairies, elves, dwarves, trolls, and forest guardians that are present in so many myths and stories. The hidden folk remind us of a magical time in our lives before, through cultural conditioning, we closed the veils between the worlds."

THE APU

If the curi represent the dark side of the spirit world in the Peruvian highlands (see chapter 3), the apu are beings of light, the most powerful of the nature spirits. Even though they reside in another dimension, they can intervene on behalf of humans.

In Inca mythology, *apu* was the name for mountain spirits, but the Incas also referred to the sacred mountains themselves as apus or apukuna, the plural of apu in Quechua. The word has a variety of meanings beyond its spiritual significance, including rich, mighty, boss, chief, powerful and wealthy. The Incas gave the title apu to each governor of the four suyus or administrative regions of the Inca Empire.

But the primary meaning of *apu* was a sacred one and was connected to the Incas' spiritual perspective. The Incas recognized three realms: Hanaq Pacha (the upper world), Kay Pacha (the human realm) and Uku Pacha (the underworld). Since mountains rose from the human world toward Hanaq Pacha, they provided the Incas a connection to their most powerful gods.

As positive spiritual sources, the apu served as protectors, watching over their surrounding territories and protecting nearby Inca villages, including their livestock and crops. In difficult times, such as during droughts and warfare, Incas called upon the apus through offerings, such as chichi (corn beer) or coca leaves. It's also believed that on occasions human sacrifices were made to the apus. In 1995, a young woman, known as the 'Inca Ice Maiden,' was discovered on top of Mount Ampato. Because of the location of the body, it's thought that she might've been sacrificed to the Ampato apu between 1450 and 1480.

APUS TODAY

While the ancient gods and spirit beings from Greek and Roman times have faded into mythology, the apu mountain spirits are still followed in the Peruvian highlands. That's especially true in traditional communities, such as the Q'eros, the last survivors of the Inca. After the Spanish Conquest, they retreated higher into the mountains and today their villages are located at more than 14,000 feet.

Each mountain has its own spirit, or guardian being, that goes by the name of the mountain where it resided. Both the highest and the smaller peaks are venerated as *apus*. Cusco, the former Inca capital, has twelve sacred *apus*, including the towering Ausangate (20,945 ft/6,384 m), Sacsayhuamán and Salkantay. Machu Picchu is also a sacred apu as is the neighboring Huayna Picchu (8,920 ft/2,720 m).

Over the past several decades, Q'ero shamans have come down from their mountain retreat and have opened their spiritual practices to the world. In fact, Q'ero shamans hold ceremonies in darkened huts in which they call upon the apu spirits to make appearances.

One Western participant in several such ceremonies, Stella Osorojos, wrote about her experience on the Reality Sandwich blog in 2010. She said that at one end of the hut was an altar that held candles, crystals, and woven bundles containing sacred stones that represented connection with the spirit world—*apus, pachamamas* (Earth spirits), angels, elementals and *amarus* (underworld animals).

In her description of one experience in the blackened room, she heard the flapping of wings as the apus passed through the walls from different directions and into the hut. Supposedly, a breeze could even be felt from the flap of wings. Even though the *apus* couldn't be seen, they spoke in high-pitched voices. At first, Osorojos was suspicious that the shaman was creating the effects, but by her last encounter she dropped her sense of disbelief.

She wrote that the main message from the *apus* is that they are available to us. "They ask that we call on them when we need help and always approach them in the spirit of *ayni*, usually translated as 'right relationship,' a Q'ero concept that interactions should always be mutually beneficial. Ayni with all spirits, be they angels, *apus, pachamamas*, ETs, and not least our fellow human beings—now that is something I believe in."

APU AS GUIDE

Michael, an American who lives in Peru, wrote about a shamanic journey he took with an apu to the realm of souls. In a lengthy e-mail to writer Linda Moulton Howe, he recounted his experience, which became the basis of an article in NEXUS Magazine.

One day, as he embarked on a shamanic meditation that was accompanied by a drumbeat, Robert wondered where souls go after death. He called upon his *apu* spirit guide to take him there. As he deepened his meditation, the *apu* agreed and soared away. In order to follow the *apu*, he merged with another guide, the spirit of a crow. But soon the *apu* was moving so fast that it was difficult for the crow and Robert to keep pace.

He noted that an *apu* can take on a variety of shapes and this one appeared to him as a gigantic salamander. "As we left this planet, I could see Earth quickly disappearing. Then it was like a sea filled with stars and galaxies fading away at a fantastic rate as the *apu* went ever faster."

After that, he found himself in a black void, then he struck a wall of energy. He and the crow followed the *apu* through the barrier, hoping not to lose sight of the spirit being. Finally, they arrived at an "immense swirl of energy...like a billion times a billion fireflies."

The *apu* told him that these points of light were soul energies in their natural state, and they were capable of creating a world where they could communicate with other souls. When Robert noticed there was a stream of these energies coming in and others leaving, he was told that some were coming from worlds where they had incarnated, and others were leaving to incarnate in a physical world.

He found it all incredibly beautiful and sensed a feeling of love that was beyond description. In this realm of the souls, there was no good or evil.

Robert's shamanic journey is a fascinating tale. But his description of his *apu* as a salamander-like being raises the possibility that rather than an *apu* he was engaged with an elemental being. Or was it an *apu* masquerading as an elemental?

THE ELEMENTALS

FIRE ELEMENTALS

Fire elementals are considered the most powerful of the elementals, and are portrayed as salamanders. They control the realm of 'fiery' emotions, such as passion, anger and love. Beings of great energy, salamanders can consume life or return life to things that have died. Paracelsus wrote: "Salamanders have been seen in the shape of fiery balls, or tongues of fire, running over fields, or peering in houses."

While they're considered friendly to those who respect them, beware of their fiery temper and their ability to entrance you with their alluring dance.

WATER ELEMENTALS

Known as Undines, water elementals are not only graceful and emotional, but also willing to help humans. They control the waters of the planet, and reside in underwater caves, lakes, rivers, marshlands and waterfalls. Many Undines in folk tales are said to be the wandering spirits of forlorn women whose endless tears over lost love fill the oceans.

While they sometimes take the form of mermaids, most Undines appear as women, albeit garbed in clothing made from seaweed. Supposedly, if a Undine bears the child of a man, she will gain a soul, and live a mortal life. And she can probably dispense with her seaweed rags.

EARTH ELEMENTALS

Known as Gnomes, earth elementals are often confused with elves, dwarves and goblins. Ugly and mischievous, these creatures stand a mere twelve to eighteen inches tall. They dress in green and brown clothing that allows them to blend into their forest surroundings.

Gnomes are caretakers of soil, rocks and trees, and are said to be immensely knowledgeable. 'Gnome actually comes from the Latin word gnoma meaning knowledge. Paracelsus claimed that earth elementals "can be seen scampering out of holes in the stumps of trees and sometimes they vanish by actually dissolving into the tree itself."

AIR ELEMENTALS

Called Sylphs in mythology, air elementals are tiny angelic-like beings with large wings. Not to be confused with fairies or cherubs, Sylphs usually live high atop tall mountains, flying among the clouds. When they land, they sometimes take the form of humans. They're known for leaving circles in the grass where they have been dancing.

Their connection with the air is said to inspire humans, endowing them with creativity. Although seemingly sympathetic to humans, Sylphs can generate storms instantly, blowing ships off course and destroying buildings.

DEVAS & FINDHORN

Deva is a Sanskrit term meaning 'shining one,' and describes any benevolent supernatural being, especially those related to nature.

While the beings are part of the vast pantheon of spirits in Hinduism, devas were virtually unknown in the West until an unusual garden came into being in northern Scotland.

Peter and Eileen Cady had been on a spiritual quest for years when they settled in the corner of an aged, rundown caravan park in northern Scotland. They did so because they were jobless and had nowhere else to go. But they also felt that they were being directed to this windswept, sandy and decidedly unappealing locale.

In spite of that humble beginning in1963, the Caddys and their companion Dorothy MacLean developed an astonishing garden by working with nature spirits that communicated with Dorothy. She called them devas or angels, and used the terms interchangeably.

Within a few years, Findhorn became famous for its enormous vegetables—such as 42-pound cabbages—grown in a difficult environment with the help of nature spirits. That phenomenon lasted a few years, but the garden continues to this day. "We were told that this was necessary as a demonstration of the power of the people and an example of what we could achieve by cooperating with the nature realms," wrote David Coates, a public relations person for the community, in an interview for the on-line magazine, Spirit of Maat.

MESSAGES

In her book, *To Hear the Angels Sing*, Dorothy Maclean says:

"I had never set out to learn to talk with angels, nor had I ever imagined that such contact could be possible or useful. Yet, when this communication began to occur, it did so in a way that I could not dispute….The garden was planted on sand in conditions that offered scant hospitality….However, through my telepathic contact with the angelic Beings who overlight and direct plant growth, specific instructions and spiritual assistance were given."

The garden that came into being astonished soil experts and horticulturists who were unable to find any explanation for it. Dorothy wrote that they "eventually had to accept the unorthodox interpretation of angelic help."

Here's the first message Dorothy receive in 1963 while meditating.

The forces of nature are something to be felt into, to be reached out to. One of the jobs for you as my free child is to sense the Nature forces such as the wind, to perceive its essence and purpose for me, and to be positive and harmonize with that essence.

When she related the insight to Peter Cady, he thought they should apply that idea to their garden. Dorothy then received this message:

Yes, you can cooperate in the garden. Begin by thinking about the nature spirits, the higher overlighting nature spirits, and tune into them. That will be so unusual as to draw their interest here. They will be overjoyed to find some members of the human race eager for their help.

THE DEVA EFFECT

In *The Faces of Findhorn,* David Spangler describes devas as living forces of creative intelligence that work behind the scene. "The devic or angelic beings work at that level where the divine image or idea is sketched out into the archetypal patterns for all forms. The devas...hold these archetypes in consciousness, wielding and patterning the forces which vivify the physical form and stepping these energies down to the elementals or nature spirits, the 'blue collar workers' who build the forms through which Spirit reveals itself."

The devas not only influenced the garden, but also the gardeners. One member of the community recalls her experience. "When I came to Findhorn in 1971 I began to realize that I was experiencing a broadening of perception; it was as though my physical senses were being extended in a way that's very hard to describe. Walking through the central garden, I experienced an extraordinary sense of being greeted and caressed by presences there that seemed to be connected with the flowers. Later that winter I came to follow up that contact with the nature kingdoms when Dorothy asked me to try illustrating her messages from the Devas.

"For me that whole period was like a sensitization process leading me into a whole different area of communication, a way of perceiving too subtle to say it was through images or sound but rather a direct reception of the essence of another being inside my own essence."

Next, we'll take a closer look at various means of making contact with the spirit world when seeking guidance.

13

MAKING CONTACT

You don't necessarily need to go to a medium to make contact with a spirit guide or deceased loved ones. There are ways, that with practice and patience, you can get a message from the other side.

DREAMS

Some dreams are reflections of happenings in your everyday life, but others allow you to escape the everyday world. Your mind is freed, allowing you to move closer to the other side. In such dreams, the non-physical becomes more real, the spirit world a short trip from your bed...at least until you wake up. Supposedly, deceased friends and relatives can make contact much easier in the dream state than when you are awake.

Of course, there is a difference between simply dreaming of someone who is dead and contacting that person's spirit in the dream state. Those who believe they have made such contact while dreaming report a sense of exhilaration and a crisp clarity in the dream environment. It's something they don't forget.

Often these connections are made close to the person's death, and the person who just recently was ill-unto-death often looks surprising healthy. The spirit might seem somewhat confused by his or her situation, and unwilling to move on, preferring to stay close to what is familiar, living humans and the Earth plane. Mediums say that typically within a few days the spirit moves to the light.

As the dreamer in such a scenario, you might be so impressed by the experience that you want to repeat it. Dream researchers say that it's possible to incubate dreams. In other words, you can request a dream about a particular concern before going to sleep.

If you attempt to make contact this way, make sure that you have a reason for doing so. Don't do it just as an experiment or for entertainment. That would be like calling up a friend who lives a thousand miles away and requesting the person to drop everything and come for a visit immediately, but for no particular reason. A spirit, especially one who is recently dead, needs to move on and not be pulled back to this world over and over again by grieving family and friends or someone who is simply curious.

That said, if you have a particular need to make contact, prepare yourself before bed by gazing at a picture of the person or reading something written by him or her. Create an image of the person in your mind and recall a pleasant event that you experienced with the deceased friend or family member. Focus for at least five or ten minutes. Then tell the person you would like to see him or her in your dreams. Think of an important question you would like answered and pose it. That will encourage the person to return with an answer. Try to make it a question that only this person can answer. Repeat it a few times, focusing your attention on the question and the person. Then let it go. Release it.

Then as you're falling asleep, tell yourself that you'll wake up after your dream and remember it. It's best to have a notebook and pen at your bedside, and jot down your dreams immediately. Even though a dream of a deceased family member or friend might seem unforgettable at 3 a.m., you might not remember all the details when you wake up hours later.

Connie Cannon, a retired nurse who resides in St. Augustine, Florida, offered this astonishing spirit contact experience related to a dream.

"While brushing my teeth recently, I accidentally knocked one of my front lower teeth with the brush. The tooth was traumatized and very painful for several days and moved anytime I ate or spoke.

"My husband's partner in his dental lab was a dentist. Dr. S was 'family' for twenty-five years, a wonderfully gifted healing physician. He passed away a few years ago. When the tooth kept hurting, I called for Dr. S and asked if he could please come and help me. Well, that night I dreamed about him.

"In the dream he was pulling that tooth. About 3 a.m. I woke up and noticed the tooth wasn't hurting. I put my finger in my mouth and didn't feel the tooth. I discovered it was lying in the front of my mouth. There was no pain whatsoever. I took the tooth out and laid it on the bedside table, then got up to check for bleeding, because I bleed easily. When I turned on the light and looked, the entire tooth, root and all, had been removed, and there was not a single drop of blood, and not a smidgen of pain!

"No doubt in my mind, none whatsoever, that Dr. S actually pulled that tooth and then awakened me so I wouldn't swallow it! Our front teeth have very deeply embedded roots and are difficult to extract. But Dr. S has enormous energy. Grateful doesn't even begin to express my feelings. What a gift of healing from a loving Spirit!"

MEDITATION

Another means of making spirit contact on your own is through meditation. Find a comfortable place to sit, preferably a location where you are alone and without distractions. Take a few deep breaths to begin and feel your body relaxing. Let your eyelids get heavy. Your brain waves are entering the alpha state, which is just above the sleep state but below full waking consciousness.

The process for connecting with a spirit is similar to the one described above for making contact through dreams. However, once you have focused on the spirit you want to contact, you remain seated and relaxed. Release the image, quiet your mind. Focus on your breath, or repeat the name of the person, as if it were a mantra, and wait for an image to appear. Be patient. It may take several sessions before you glimpse an image or hear a familiar voice.

If the person you are seeking in spirit doesn't come to you after several tries, it could be that the spirit isn't interested in making an appearance at this time. If that's the case, you might try to contact a spirit guide without attaching a name or face. Pose a question you want answered, focus on it, then release it, send it out and wait for a response.

Here's a story about spirit contact through meditation that Mike Perry of Cornwall, England wrote about on his blog.

"Last night I was meditating, nothing unusual there, though usually I meditate in the mornings. My wife had gone up to bed and I just had a feeling that I needed to meditate. I remember checking the clock and telling myself that twenty minutes would suffice.

"I followed my usual routine and after about 15 minutes I heard a voice in my left ear. This has never happened previously. The voice simply said, *Your dad is listening to you.*

"It was absolutely clear, though I didn't recognize the voice. I was still relaxed in my meditation pose so I followed my instinct and spoke softly, telling my dad how I missed him and my mother, and said a thank you for all they did for me over the years, especially while I was growing up. I also spoke about my son and how he was doing.

"I then opened my eyes. I can only think it goes back to the time when my dad died and how, regrettably, I wasn't there. It's something I've always had on my mind, even though he moved on over twenty years ago.

"As for the voice I heard, I'm not sure what to believe. Maybe, as it was late at night, I had simply fallen asleep and dreamt it, but I'm pretty sure I didn't. I'd like to think that dad heard what I said."

AUTOMATIC WRITING

Here's another technique for making spirit contact, this one through a combination of meditation and handwriting. It's best to enter a relaxed, meditative state with your arms resting on a desk or table. You will need paper and a pen in front of you. Hold the pen in your hand over the paper. Don't ask any questions. When automatic writing begins, it will feel as if your hand is moving on its own accord. You might also feel exhilarated.

Supposedly, the material comes from an outside source—spirit contact—and not the unconscious mind of the meditator. Typically, the meditator is unaware of what is being written. You might try to shift the focus from your left-brain logical thinking to right-brain intuitive thinking by turning your attention to something else, such as watching television or reading e-mail. When your hand starts to move, don't try to judge the quality or nature of what you are writing. It might be incoherent or illegible without proper grammar or punctuation. Consider it preparation. Now you're ready to pose a question.

If your hand doesn't move after a few minutes, take a break and try again. Make sure that you are relaxed and in a receptive mood. It might take several attempts before you succeed. You might find it surprising that numerous books have been written via automatic writing. In 1916, Carl Jung channeled a spirit guide named Basilides of Alexandria and wrote a detailed spiritual text called Seven Sermons of the Dead over three evenings. Basilides was a real person, born in Syria, who became a teacher in Alexandria in 133-155 AD.

Words, thoughts, and ideas came to Jung as Basilides dictated. Jung transcribed several commentaries by Basilides speaking to the dead. The text emphasizes human individuality. Basilides explained that upon death we maintain the fullness of our individuality rather than being absorbed into the Oneness.

It's impossible to discern how much of this text came from Jung's unconscious mind and how much, if any, came from an outside source. However, from this experience, Jung formulated the concept of the collective unconscious. He considered it part of the evolutionary process common to all people and distinct from individual consciousness. He believed it was the foundation of what the ancients called the 'sympathy of all things,' which is a way of saying that everyone and every thing is interconnected.

OUIJA BOARD

The board is a medium of communication, like automatic writing. But typically it takes two people with their fingertips on the planchette, which moves across the board spelling out words. At first, the movement will probably be slow, the process tedious, and the message, if any, confusing. But with practice, especially if the same two people are involved, the movement of the planchette might become smooth and swift and the messages clear and understandable.

But where is the information coming from and how reliable is it? Skeptics believe the planchette moves through unconscious muscle movements and that there's nothing otherworldly about it. At the other extreme of skepticism are people who believe that dabbling with a Ouija board will attract evil spirits intent on deception and abuse.

Proponents say that you can contact entities of equal or higher vibration than yourself and receive useful information. But you can also get nonsense or threatening comments from mischievous lower entities. That's especially true if you don't take the communication seriously or you're looking for a thrill rather than wisdom or knowledge.

Well known writers who have received spiritual and philosophic writings through the Ouija board include Jane Roberts, who started using the board with her husband, Rob, and went on to trance-channeling. She wrote *The Seth Material* and many other books that were supposedly transmitted to her from a spirit guide named Seth while she was in a trance. Similarly, Esther and Jerry Hicks first contacted Abraham through the Ouija board before Esther began dictating messages from Abraham—a collective of spirits—and writing a series of books on the law of attraction, as well as holding workshops.

PATIENCE WORTH

She was supposedly a spirit contacted through a Ouija board by Pearl Lenore Curran beginning in 1913. If true—and there were many witnesses—Patience Worth authored several novels, poetry and prose, delivered initially by way of the board, and then through her typewriter. When asked when she lived, Patience Worth gave the dates 1649 and 1694 in Dorsetshire, England.

Pearl Curran was a St. Louis, Missouri housewife with limited education when a friend convinced her to try the Ouija board with her. At first, when the planchette moved, it only spelled out garble and Pearl found it boring. But it all changed when a clear message came though. "Many moons ago I lived. Again I come. Patience Worth is my name," it spelled out.

Eventually, the messages came faster and faster and finally Pearl realized that the words were coming into her mind at the same time, and that she no longer needed the Ouija board. From then on, for the next 25 years she dictated the transmissions, or wrote them out herself. Pearl would usually just sit in a brightly lit room with her notebook or typewriter and when the messages began to come to her, she would start writing. The stories included words and phrases from ancient languages, and the mention of things that had not been in use for hundreds of years and more. Much of it seemed out of the realm of Pearl's knowledge, making the nature of her literary accomplishments especially mysterious.

14

TECHNOLOGY & SPIRIT CONTACT

Thomas Edison is best known as the inventor of the phonograph, the motion picture camera, and a long-lasting electric light bulb. But he didn't stop there. The prolific inventor held 1,093 U.S. patents. In spite of the many practical, every day applications of his genius, he also had a life-long fascination with the after-life. And, as a scientist, he always tried to apply science and technology to his experiments in spirit contact.

In his twenties, for example, he searched for an unknown force that explained supernatural phenomena. Eventually, he abandoned his investigation of the mysterious 'Odic force,' and moved on to other matters. But his interest in supernatural never faded, and finally in the last decade of his life he experimented with what became known as the 'Telephone to the Dead.'

"Now what I propose to do is furnish psychic investigators with an apparatus which will give a scientific aspect to their work," Edison wrote in an essay in 1920. "For my part, I am inclined to believe that our personality hereafter will be able to affect matter. If this reasoning be correct, then, if we can evolve an instrument so delicate as to be affected, or moved, or manipulated—whichever term you want to use—by our personality as it survives in the next life, such an instrument, when made available, ought to record something."

It was Edison's way of dealing with the question of life after death. He theorized that 'life units' unknown by science joined together to create every animate (and possibly inanimate) object. Upon death, these life units broke up into their respective individual units and joined another form after human death. Edison was convinced that swarms of life units were responsible for not only the thinking and memory of humans, but for every life function of every plant and animal. His evidence that swarms of life units were responsible for memory consisted of the fact that someone can burn their fingertips badly enough to remove all the skin in a blister, but yet, the fingerprint whorls would grow back the same way.

In his essays, the device he was working on was likened to a valve that would amplify the ability for the swarms to manipulate the object so that "it does not matter how slight is the effort, it will be sufficient to record whatever there is to be recorded."

Following his death, the Edison Estate, protective of his legacy, removed 80 pages from his diary that discussed spiritualism. Although Edison proposed in an essay that a recently deceased colleague would be the first spirit to attempt to contact him, neither Edison's plans for the inter-dimensional communication device or a model—if one existed - has ever been revealed to the public.

ELECTRONIC VOICE PHENOMENON

In the decades after Thomas Edison's death, other researchers have continued his work to contact the dead through electronic devices. In fact, a field of research has developed known as Electronic Voice Phenomenon (EVP) or Instrumental Transcommunication (ITC).

Friedrich Jurgenson, a Swede, is considered the first person to record mysterious voices. He did so while attempting to capture birdsongs. In this book *Voices From Space*, he contended that these voices were not from living beings, but they were actually the voices of the dead.

Dr. Konstantin Raudive, a German psychologist and student of Carl Jung, read Jurgenson's book and decided to investigate his claims that he recorded the voices of dead family members and well known people, including Hitler and Goring. On the day they met in April 1965, Jurgenson plugged a microphone into a recorder and Raudive took part in his first EVP recording session.

He recalled that he clearly heard the word "nonsense" in response to his statement that inhabitants of the world of spirit were living a carefree life. This session peaked Raudive's interest in the paranormal. He worked with Jurgenson for a short time, then continued the exploration on his own. Over the course of the next three years, Dr. Raudive collected over 72,000 distinct voices recorded during his sessions. In 1972, he published *"Breakthrough:*

An Amazing Experiment in Electronic Communication with the Dead."

Raudive died two years later, but according to other researchers that didn't stop him from continuing his experiments from the other side. One EVP investigator called out Raudive's name three times during a session after he had finished reading *Breakthrough* and was greeted with the words, "It's Konstantin!"

New digital devices have been developed in recent years to pursue electronic voice phenomena. The so-called Ghost Box, created by a paranormal researcher from Colorado, uses 'radio sweep' technology. The device sweeps across radio broadcasts producing a stream of bits of human speech, music, and white noise. Researchers believe that spirits somehow use this raw audio to verbally communicate.

Skeptics, however, say that these researchers are finding meaning in sounds to suit their beliefs that it's possible for the dead to talk to us. They contend that if randomly selected listeners heard the so-called communications, they would not hear the words the investigators claimed were on the recordings.

Frank Sumption, who created the Ghost Box, is unfazed by such criticism. In fact, he doubles down, saying that his Ghost Box was developed with the help of dead scientists who spoke to him in earlier EVP experiments. Christopher Moon, editor of *Haunted Times Magazine,* is impressed by his work and says Frank Sumption has completed Thomas Edison's Telephone to the Dead.

PHOTOGRAPHING ORBS

Circles of light called orbs that appear on photographs are the atmosphere's equivalent to the crop circles of the earth. Skeptics point out there is no scientific evidence that crop circles are made by non-humans forces and there's no evidence that spirits create orbs on photos. On the other hand, just because humans create some crop circles doesn't mean they are all created by people, and just because some orbs are created by moisture, dust or reflections, doesn't mean that all orbs can be accounted for by such everyday mechanisms.

One point of view suggests there is nothing mysterious about either phenomena; the other says that when you discard the explainable crop circles or orb photos, a mystery remains.

Clearly, of all the evidence presented in support of the reality of spirit contact, the topic of orbs is probably the most contentious. For skeptics, it's obvious that such 'specters' are explainable glitches in the photographic process that occur under certain atmospheric conditions—moisture or dust in the air, lens flares, or reflections—especially with digital cameras.

On the other hand, people experienced in taking and analyzing orb photos say they can easily distinguish those related to atmospheric conditions from those that seem to represent a form of conscious energy.

Many who believe some orbs on photos represent spirits of the dead are people who accept the reality of other paranormal phenomena and consider themselves as spiritual rather than religious. That said, it's easy to conjecture that the orb-believing crowd are not highly scientific folks. Ironically, one of the strongest advocate of the reality of orbs as conscious energy is a physicist, Klaus Heinemann, who has published 60 peer reviewed papers in his field and has worked with NASA. He has also co-authored two books on orbs and participated in a documentary film called, *Orbs: The Veil is Lifting.*

Describing his first book, Heinemann said, *The Orb Project* demonstrates that our conventional physical reality is merely an extension of the limitless spiritual dimension, and that orbs are connected with realities outside of our normal human perception." That concept fits well with a popular New Age sentiment that goes like this: *We are not physical beings seeking a spiritual experience, but rather are spiritual beings experiencing a human existence.*

In spite of Heinemann's credentials, skeptics are not impressed and reviewing their comment on the Internet one word stands out when addressing the spiritual nature of orbs: *Nonsense.* "A non-mysterious phenomena," one skeptic wrote on a blog.

Noting such points of view, James O'Dea, president, Institute of Noetic Sciences, wrote: "Breakthroughs in science come when we are prepared to explore persistent anomalies. Orbs may just be evidence that can only be explained outside of the box of current limiting and reductionist worldviews."

The nature of orbs is likely to remain a controversial topic, one that sharply divides believers in spirits and an afterworld, and those who are confident that dust is the final solution.

15

GUARDIAN ANGELS

No offense to your deceased friends or family members, but they are not angels. So who or what are angels?

The word 'angel' actually comes from the Greek word *aggelos*, which means messenger. Likewise, the Hebrew word mal'ak often translates to 'angel' and the primary meaning is messenger. The image that comes to mind are winged figures from biblical stories, where angels are categorized in three groups as (1) Seraphim, Cherubim, and Thrones; (2) the Dominations, Virtues, and Powers; (3) the Principalities, Archangels, and Angels.

They are supposedly other dimensional beings who have never lived as humans. Yet, according to legend and belief, they are also active in the physical world, and supposedly can take on a physical form. If you find yourself in a precarious situation and are assisted or protected by someone who seemingly appears out of nowhere and disappears again, it could mean that you were helped by an angel. You might think of that person as an angel metaphorically, even if you don't believe in angels!

If you had such an angel experience, your angel probably didn't have wings. Does that mean that the wings were just a way of distinguishing these benevolent beings from spirit guides or other entities? Yes and no, says Morgana Starr, author of Angel Whispers.

"The angels show themselves in a way we can understand. Since they have the ability of 'flight'—being anywhere they need to be at a moment's notice—they show us what we understand—wings." Other times, she notes, they move incognito—appearing wingless— among us to complete their appointed tasks.

A medium who resides in central Florida, Morgana says she

works with the archangel Anael, who she says carries the energy of the Feminine Divine—the Mother aspect of god. Morgana's description of Anael's wings is surprisingly complex. "The major set of wings are two pair—one white pair to lift her up and one black pair to cover her like a cloak for comfort. She also has smaller sets of wings at her ankles, her knees and shoulders, and another set at her head. The smaller sets have a golden sheen and are used to hover....buzzing at incredible speed, creating a golden glow."

While Morgana says that Anael has displayed her wings to her, the medium recognizes that what she saw was, in a sense, an illusion: "If human eyes were to really see the form of an angel, as it is, they would be blinded. Similarly, an angel's natural voice is of such a high vibration that it would burst all the vessels in a human body."

Marcus Anthony, an Australian futurist, intuitive counselor and author, says the human mind adjusts to what it encounters. "The deeper human psyche does not perceive through the body and five senses during mystical experiences." Rather, the events are comprehended "according to the existing perceptual framework of the individual."

He notes that entities will often be perceived or represented within the mind according to what's the best fit. "A being of great love and radiance may be seen as Jesus, if that is the person's best frame of reference. But this is not simply a projection of the mind. The being exists independently of the person perceiving it, but the person has a limited capacity to understand what he or she is seeing."

THE SCIENTIST & THE ANGELS

Neurologists diagnose, treat, and study conditions that affect the brain and the entire nervous system, and by the very nature of their profession, they tend to be skeptical about claims that separate human consciousness from the brain. Typically, they espouse a materialistic view emphasizing that the brain is the source of consciousness. In that sense, near-death experiences (NDEs) and related visions, such as spirit contact, are products of the dying brain—hallucinations that stop when the brain's activity ceases. If this hypothesis is true, then NDEs tell us nothing about life after death, or the reality of spirits encountered in such experiences.

Now comes Dr. Eben Alexander, a Harvard-educated neurosurgeon, who drifted in a coma for seven days in 2008 after contracting meningitis. During his illness Alexander says that the part of his brain that controls human thought and emotion "shut down" and that he experienced "something so profound that it gave me a scientific reason to believe in consciousness after death."

What was it? He saw angels.

Writing for Newsweek, Alexander says he was met by a beautiful blue-eyed woman in a "place of clouds, big fluffy pink-white ones" and "shimmering beings." He has written a book, *Proof of Heaven*, describing his experience. "Birds? Angels? These words registered later, when I was writing down my recollections. But neither of these words do justice to the beings themselves, which were quite simply different from anything I have known on this planet. They were more advanced. Higher forms."

Alexander added that a "huge and booming...glorious chant, came down from above, and I wondered if the winged beings were producing it. The sound was palpable and almost material, like a rain that you can feel on your skin but doesn't get you wet."

The neurosurgeon says he had heard stories from patients who spoke of out-of-body experiences, but disregarded them as "wishful thinking." Now he has reconsidered his opinion following his own experience. "I know full well how extraordinary, how frankly unbelievable, all this sounds. Had someone, even a doctor, told me a story like this in the old days, I would have been quite certain that they were under the spell of some delusion. But what happened to me was, far from being delusional, as real or more real than any event in my life. That includes my wedding day and the birth of my two sons."

He added: "I've spent decades as a neurosurgeon at some of the most prestigious medical institutions in our country. I know that many of my peers hold to the theory that the brain, and in particular the cortex, generates consciousness and that we live in a universe devoid of any kind of emotion, much less the unconditional love...."

Now Alexander dismisses such skepticism. "But that belief, that theory, now lies broken at our feet. What happened to me destroyed it."

Alexander, it seems, has heard the call and is sending out a message of universal love. Whether we listen or not, whether we accept it or not, is up to us.

PART THREE
ALIEN ABDUCTIONS

16

THE HILL ABDUCTION

When it comes to things that go bump in the night, the idea of being abducted by alien beings, taken aboard a craft, and examined on a table is so frightening and outrageous that many of us don't want to believe that such a thing could happen. But Betty Hills insists it did for her, and for many others in the years that followed. Here's her story.

The night of September 19, 1961 was cold in the White Mountains of New Hampshire. Betty and Barney Hill were headed home to Portsmouth after vacationing in Canada. In spite of the darkness and the terrain, which reaches altitudes of greater than 6,200 feet, Betty, a 41-year-old teacher and Barney, a 39-year-old post worker, knew the way. They had driven it many times. They were making the trip at night due to reports that Hurricane Esther, an intense Category 4 storm with winds of 145 miles per hour, might take a swipe at New England.

They passed through customs on the Canadian/U.S. border around nine that evening and half an hour or so later, reached the town of Colebrook. From there, it was 170 miles along Route 3 to Portsmouth. They figured that Colebrook would probably be their last chance for coffee and a bite to eat, so they stopped at a nearly deserted restaurant.

As they sat at the restaurant counter—Barney with a hamburger and Betty enjoying a slice of chocolate cake—neither of them had any inkling that their lives were about to change forever. Neither of them knew they were about to become the modern era's first alien abductees.

They left the restaurant at 10:05 p.m., which meant they would arrive home around 2:30 or 3:00 a.m. Route 3 was two lanes and well-paved, but it climbed and twisted into steep mountains and didn't invite speeding. Barney was at the wheel, Betty in the passenger seat, and the couple's dachshund, Delsey, was asleep at Betty's feet. The night was clear, and the moon bright, nearly full.

Around 10:15, Betty noticed a large star that seemed to be growing brighter and larger. She watched it for several minutes, then drew Barney's attention to it. As they continued to watch it, they speculated about what it might be—a planet, a plane, a satellite. They stopped along the side of the road several times to watch the light with a pair of binoculars. Delsey started whimpering and crying and at one point Betty returned to the car with the dog. She was now convinced the light was not only moving, but was following them.

Barney, on the other hand, kept telling himself it had to be a military plane and apparently became irritated with Betty for not accepting an ordinary explanation. By the time the light was just several hundred feet above them, Barney stopped again. The light dropped lower and he got out of the car. He saw a tremendous object and a double row of windows.

"Barney was fully gripped with fear now, but for a reason that he cannot yet explain, he found himself moving across the road on the driver's side of the car, on to the field, and across the field, directly toward it," wrote John G. Fuller in *The Interrupted Journey: Two Lost Hours Aboard a Flying Saucer.*

Betty was still in the car, screaming at Barney to return. They were parked in the middle of the highway and even though there wasn't any traffic, she worried about it and worried even more that Barney wasn't answering her. She was about two hundred feet away from Barney, but he didn't seem to hear her. He stood in the field, the binoculars pressed to his eyes. And what he saw terrified him—the figures of at least half a dozen beings that "seemed to be bracing themselves against the transparent windows, as the craft tilted down toward his direction," wrote Fuller.

When all but one of the half dozen figures disappeared from the window, the lone crew member peered down at Barney. He had never seen eyes like this before and tore back across the field, screaming.

The Hills' experience that night was to become the first known abduction of humans by small gray beings with large black eyes. Now, more than a half century later, it remains the most famous case. In the realm of UFOs and aliens, only the purported Roswell crash is better known.

MISSING TIME

On their way home, Betty and Barney suddenly realized they were 35 miles from where they had been moments ago. They pulled up in front of their home at dawn, and later realized a trip that should have taken them four hours had taken more than six and they couldn't account for at least two hours.

But they couldn't helping wandering if the lost time was somehow related to their UFO encounter.

AFTERMATH

In late December 1963, more than two years after their mysterious experience, the Hills consulted Dr. Benjamin Simon, a psychiatrist. They subsequently began a series of hypnotic regressions in an attempt to fully recall what had happened to them.

By this time, they had been interviewed by Major Paul W. Henderson of Pease Air Force Base, where Betty initially filed a report about their sighting; by Walter Webb, a scientific advisor to the National Investigations Committee on Aerial Phenomenon (NICAP); and by other military personnel. They had been living with an almost constant anxiety about the events of September 19, and had done their best to recall everything they had seen and had even drawn separate sketches of the craft. But their amnesia about the missing two hours had persisted.

By the summer of 1962, Barney was experiencing profound exhaustion, had developed high blood pressure and ulcers, and his doctor referred him to a psychiatrist, Dr. Duncan Stephens. For the next year, he and Stephens explored Barney's relationship with his two sons, who lived in Philadelphia with their mother. Barney felt this was the basis of his problem and that the events of September 19, 1961 were tangential. Betty suffered less anxiety than Barney, but was haunted by a series of vivid, detailed dreams she'd had ten days after the event. The dreams had continued for five nights, then stopped, but were more like memories.

Stephens eventually referred Barney to Dr. Simon for hypnotic regression. At the end of the first session, it was obvious to Dr. Simon that Barney had suffered profound emotional trauma related to an experience with an unidentified flying object that was either real or perceived to be real. But the second regression veered into a purported abduction, an area that Simon considered to be less probable and probably not real. Rather than proceeding with a third regression with Barney, he decided to regress Betty.

Fuller's book includes the harrowing transcripts of these regression sessions. In Betty's session, she describes a pregnancy test that was conducted on her—a long needle inserted through her navel. It sounds similar to amniocentesis, where a small amount of fluid is taken from the amniotic sac surrounding a developing fetus and the fetal DNA is examined for genetic abnormalities. But this procedure wasn't known in 1961 and didn't come into widespread use until the late 1980s. Research on abductees in the decades since the Hills' experience suggests that the culling of ova and sperm is common, but back in the early sixties, there was no precedent for what Betty described during her session.

During Betty's second session, Simon gave her a post-hypnotic suggestion that she would be able to sketch a "star map" that the leader on the craft had shown her. When she eventually did so, her drawing depicted twelve prominent stars and three smaller, dimmer stars. Lines and dashes connected the stars. The solid, heavy lines were trade routes, the other solid lines were places the craft traveled occasionally, and the broken lines - the dashes— represented expeditions.

In 1968, an elementary school teacher and amateur astronomer, Marjorie Fish, began studying Betty's star map to find out if it was possible to determine the star system from which the UFO originated. She constructed a three-dimensional model of nearby sun-like stars using thread and beads. Fish wasn't able to figure it out until 1969, when the Gliese Star Catalogue was published.

The Gliese is a modern star catalogue of stars located within 25 parasecs of Earth. One parasec is roughly 3.26 light years or about 19 trillion miles. Fish studied thousands of vantage points and finally determined that the best match was a double star system,

Zeta Reticuli, and concluded that the craft that had abducted the Hills may have originated on a planet orbiting that star system.

Carl Sagan and most other scientists dismissed Fish's research. But Walter Mitchell, an astronomer and professor at Ohio State University, believed Fish's calculations were correct. "The pattern discovered by Marjorie Fish has an uncanny resemblance to the map drawn by Betty Hill," he wrote in the December 1974 issue of *Astronomy Magazine*. "The stars are mostly the ones we would visit if we were exploring from Zeta Reticuli. The travel patterns make sense."

In mid-March 1986, my wife Trish and I covered a UFO conference in Hollywood, Florida for *OMNI* Magazine. The featured speakers were author and researcher Budd Hopkins and Betty Hill. Our editor was interested in articles on both of them for the magazine's Anti-Matter section, which featured articles about UFOs and the paranormal.

The conference hadn't been well advertised and only about a hundred people attended, making it easy for the attendees and speakers to mingle. Betty was the first speaker and the crowd was riveted by her story. In her soft, gravelly voice, she took us back to that night twenty-five years earlier, her hands gesturing constantly, sometimes trembling. She paced back and forth in front of the podium as she spoke, her body imbued with a restless energy, and puffed frequently on a cigarette. She spoke fast, with passion and resolve, answered questions, and all the while her pale blue eyes flicked from the crowd to the windows, as though she expected to see something in that vast sweep of blue March sky.

After her talk, we sat outside with Betty and Budd Hopkins. Betty was 67 then, had traveled to the conference with a friend, and we invited them both to our townhouse for an interview the next evening. It was obvious to anyone who talked to Betty, who heard her speak, that something had happened to her and Barney that cold September night in 1961. The events had profoundly impacted her life. But an abduction by aliens? By small, frail-looking beings with large black eyes and over sized bald heads? Beings that had performed medical experiments on her and Barney? That had taken ovum from her and sperm from Barney? It strained credulity.

In retrospect, though, the abduction phenomenon didn't reach a tipping point in the public consciousness until the publication of two books in 1987—Budd Hopkins' *Intruders* and Whitley Strieber's *Communion*. Both books became bestsellers and dealt with alien abductions, primarily by Grays—the same entities that Betty and Barney Hill had encountered. But in March 1986, those books lay months in the future.

After the conference the next day, Betty and her friend followed us to our place. We sat in the living room for a couple of hours, Betty entertaining us with stories about the numerous UFO sightings she'd had since she and Barney were abducted. She had a quick laugh and a terrific sense of humor. But when she described the particulars of what had happened to her and Barney, her merriment instantly vanished. She talked in fits and starts, as if she couldn't spit the words out fast enough.

There were eleven Grays—a leader, who seemed to be in charge and the only one who 'spoke' English; the examiner—the Gray who conducted the tests; and nine other crew members. She and Barney were examined in separate rooms and samples of their hair, fingernails, and skin were taken, and their eyes, ears, nose, and throat were examined. When Betty's examiner brought out an instrument with a long needle and she was told it would be inserted through her navel, her terror collapsed into panic, but she couldn't move, couldn't flee.

"I wanted to know what they were going to do to me. The leader explained it was a pregnancy test. I told him it would hurt." The examiner inserted the needle anyway and she squirmed in agony until the leader touched Betty's forehead and the pain stopped.

At one point, Betty was obviously overwhelmed by the memories and abruptly pushed away from the table. She headed out the sliding glass doors to the parking lot outside the townhouse and we all hurried after her. She stood in the middle of the lot, pointing overhead, her fingertip following a moving light.

"See that?" she exclaimed. "See that light?"

We saw a distant moving light and figured it was an plane. Betty's friend voiced what we were thinking, but Betty shook her head. "They're masters of camouflage."

Maybe they are. Who can say for sure? But the point wasn't the light—plane, satellite, UFO—it was the utter conviction and resolve with which Betty uttered those words. And right then, any doubts we had about Betty Hill vanished completely. She and Barney had experienced *something* on Route 3 that night in 1961. But what?

Whatever it was, the event defined the rest of Betty's life. Thanks to Fuller's book, an article in *Look* Magazine, and then a movie, she and Barney became internationally known as the first modern day UFO abductees.

BEYOND THE HILLS

In the decades since the alleged abduction of the Hills, UFOs and aliens have become embedded in popular culture. Through an explosion of TV shows, movies, and books, our collective consciousness is now primed for this stuff.

More abductees are coming forward with their stories, daily sightings worldwide are reported to MUFON or other organizations and often end up on You Tube, and mass sightings—like the Phoenix Lights in 1997—have become more common. Researchers with impressive credentials, like John E. Mack, M.D., a professor of psychiatry at Harvard Medical School until his death in 2004, and Dr. David Jacob, a history professor at Temple University, have regressed thousands of individuals and written books about their discoveries. Former presidents have had sightings. And some countries have released their UFO files.

And yet, the official stance of the U.S. government and of mainstream science is that none of it is real or plausible because—well, take your pick:

The distances the craft would have to travel are too great.

Extraterrestrial life hasn't been proven.

Individuals who claim to be abductees are mentally ill and the memories they recover under hypnosis are masking childhood sexual abuse.

Hypnosis is a flawed technique.

Most sightings are weather balloons, meteors, the planets Venus or Jupiter.

You get the general idea here. Fear of ridicule may be the biggest impediment to our understanding of what is actually occurring. Abductees and individuals who experience encounters are often reluctant to talk about what has happened to them for fear of losing their jobs or being ostracized by their communities, churches, even by their own families.

As Mack noted in *Abduction: Human Encounters with Aliens*, we don't know where the aliens or UFOs are coming from or whether they even originate in the physical universe. "But they manifest in the physical world and bring about definable consequences in that domain." In the aftermath of an encounter, many people suffer what Mack calls "ontological shock," where their entire worldview is shattered. As a result, encounter experiences can provide a venue for spiritual transformation.

David Jacobs, on the other hand, believes the abduction phenomenon is overwhelmingly negative and that there is an active alien hybrid breeding program underway. In his book *Secret Life— Firsthand Documented Accounts of UFO Abductions,* Jacobs concluded that hybrids or aliens will "integrate into human society and assume control…"

Today, in the second decade of the twenty-first century, anyone who experiences an encounter has an advantage that the Hills didn't—there are organizations and websites where an encounter can be reported and will be taken seriously. MUFON—Mutual UFO Network - is the largest organization of its kind, with chapters in more than twenty countries and in all fifty states. Their website: www.mufon.com. They mainly collect and report sightings, not abductions.

Author Whitley Strieber, whose 1987 bestseller *Communion* brought the abduction scenario fully into public consciousness, has one of the most comprehensive websites—www.unknowncountry. com - on unexplained phenomena. As an abductee himself, he understands the isolation and terror that experiencers go through.

Another excellent place to report sightings or encounters is the national UFO Reporting Center at http://www.nuforc.org.

17

THE M.O. OF AN ABDUCTION

When police investigate a crime, one of the first things they do is attempt to establish an M.O.—the modus operandi or method of operation. What was the nature of the crime? Where did it occur and when did it happen? Who were the perpetrators? What methods did the perpetrators employ in the execution of the crime? What actions did the perpetrator take to avoid detection? Modus operandi is also used in criminal profiling and assists in defining motives, a suspect's particular psychology, and can help to find links between crimes.

Establishing an M.O. usually involves answering the five interrogatives we all learned in elementary school: who, what, where, when, and why? With abductions though, that last question—why?—may be the most difficult to answer. Researchers have theories about why these abductions are happening and about the motives of the perpetrators. These range from a hybrid breeding program to saving the planet from destruction by humanity to forcing a paradigm shift in our world view.

Budd Hopkins believed the alien motives are evil and that they intend us harm. In his memoir, *Art, Life, and UFOs*, he said he no longer had the luxury of disbelief about whether UFOs and abductions were real. "Even back in the 1970s I felt the sense of being helpless in the face of the accumulating evidence, and aware that the UFO phenomenon made the future seem increasingly ominous."

Dr. David Jacobs, who has regressed thousands of abductees, agrees with Hopkins. In *The Threat: Revealing the Secret Alien Agenda*, Jacobs described how researchers fall into two camps—the Positives, who believe the alien intention is ultimately benevolent, and researchers like him. "Contrary to the optimistic predictions of the Positives, I do not like what I see for the future. And the more information I gather about the abduction phenomenon, the more ominous the picture looks. When the end comes—and it will come—what will happen to humanity?"

Jacobs believes the alien intentions can be narrowed to three possibilities: the actions the aliens take are mutually beneficial to both aliens and humans; they are beneficial to the aliens and deliberately harmful to humans; "or they are beneficial to the aliens who simply do not care what human consequences their actions might have."

John E Mack, by his own admission, fell into the Positive camp. In *Abduction*, he stated that his overall impression about the abduction process is that it isn't evil. "… I have the sense—might I say faith—that the abduction phenomenon is, at its core, about the preservation of life on Earth at a time when the planet's life is profoundly threatened."

Many abductees are not as sanguine as Mack. They are so severely traumatized by what happened to them that they never get over it. Rather than asking why aliens are abducting humans, their litany becomes, *Why me? Why did this happen to me?*

So, for the moment, let's set why aside and explore what, where, when, and how and see if those interrogatives shed any light on the why.

'THE CRIME SCENE'

An abduction can happen anywhere—on a highway, in the woods, in bed, in the middle of the family dinner, or in your backyard. You can be of any age, ethnicity, or religious persuasion.

Typically, the abductee may notice strange lights in the sky, as Betty Hill did, that move erratically and progressively closer to you. Or he or she awakens suddenly to see lights in the bedroom window that are abnormally bright and coming closer. Sometimes the abductee bolts out of sleep and finds several short, strange-looking entities standing around his bed. Paralysis usually follows. Even if the abductee is still conscious, he can't move. A beam of light may move him out a window, through walls and doors, and up into a waiting craft. Another variation is when the abductee suddenly finds herself on a surgical table, surrounded by Grays, and has no memory of how she got there. This scenario is what happened to Diane Fine, a lifelong abductee, in the early nineties.

Diane Fine, whom my wife and I wrote about in *Aliens in the Backyard: UFO Encounters, Abductions, & Synchronicity*, was working at a marina in California at the time. Each day, she had to climb a lot of stairs and it had affected her left knee to the point where it throbbed constantly. She was a military wife at the time, with access to health care, but had no time to visit the clinic to have the knee checked out. One night, she came awake on a surgical table. Despite the bright overhead light, she could see entities gathered at the foot of the table. The largest of the four seemed to be in charge. She realized they had operated on her knee.

"If you can fix my knee, why don't you fix my autoimmune disorder?" she asked.

One of them answered telepathically. "We can't. It's karmic. This (the knee) is mechanical."

Diane immediately lost consciousness. The next morning she checked her knee and found a small incision. It healed within a few days and the knee hasn't bothered her since. She has no recollection of how she got into the craft or left it.

Diane's experience had both positive and negative aspects. She was taken against her will, and her abductors tampered with her memory. But they also repaired her injured knee.

Connie J Cannon, a lifelong abductee like Diane Fine, can recall her abductions without hypnosis. However, with one exception, Connie doesn't know how she gets onto or off of the crafts. Such lapses in memory and consciousness are common.

In the late 1980s, when she was in her early 40s, she awakened at 3:30 one morning and realized she was standing on a street corner in her nightgown, several blocks from her home. She felt a rumbling sensation beneath her feet, as if the ground on which she stood was being torn apart by powerful forces. She knew what it meant and looked frantically around for somewhere to hide. And then she saw them—three approaching crafts that held beings she knew would control her and leave her sick and despairing.

Terrified, she tried to hide—in the shadows, the grass, the bushes, anywhere. One of the crafts separated from the other two and suddenly she was inside of it, strapped into what resembled a desk chair. She didn't have any idea how she'd gotten from the ground into the craft.

The ship seemed to move and spin simultaneously, nauseating her. When it abruptly stopped, she nearly vomited. A Gray stood in front of her, its large black eyes staring into hers, and ordered her to look down. A shield slid open under her seat, exposing a transparent floor that reminded her of a glass bottom boat she'd once ridden at Silver Springs, Florida. Something similar to an infrared light came on and she could not only see a house directly below the craft, but could see inside it—rooms, furniture, even people asleep in bed. Instead of being terrified, she became enraged. "What do you want me to see?" she demanded. "It's the middle of the night, those people are sleeping."

The Gray just stood there, staring into her eyes. Then, suddenly, it was morning and she was back in bed. She had no idea how she'd gotten from the craft to her bed. She knew it wasn't a dream, though, because when she sat up, blood poured from her right nostril and the right side of her body felt numb. As she stood, the room spun. Connie, who was an R.N., thought she might have had a stroke and shouted for her husband. By the time they reached the emergency room, she couldn't walk and he had to carry her inside.

A CAT scan didn't find anything unusual - no blood clots, aneurysm, no evidence of a stroke. But a sinus scan revealed a small anomalous shadow on the right side of her nose. She later came to believe this was an implant.

ABDUCTING CHILDREN

It seems that many of those who have experienced multiple abductions were selected as children for whatever purpose the entities have in mind. Connie has clear memories of at least three childhood abductions.

When she was four years old, she lived directly across the street from the Alabama governor's mansion in Montgomery. Her older sister was already in school and Connie wanted to look like a big girl, so she would carry a couple of books and stroll up and down on the brick wall that lined the sidewalk along the front lawn of her house.

"One morning as I was playing schoolgirl, walking along the wall and carrying the books, a very tall entity appeared at the end of the wall. It's a crystal clear memory. This being was at least seven and a half feet tall. Yes, I was little, but the entity was not human height. I knew the difference. It seemed to be male although it had blond hair that reached below its shoulders and pale white skin like an albino. He was wearing a one-piece silver-gray garment with long sleeves. That's very clear because it was so different from anything I'd ever seen."

There was no one else around. At that time, it was safe for kids to play outside without supervision. When she turned to walk in the opposite direction on the wall, the entity wrapped a long thin arm around her from behind. "I screamed, and then I was up in the air. The next memory I have is that I was back on the wall, but the books were strewn on the lawn."

That's when a woman appeared in the yard. "She came and took my hand and walked me to our door, then just seemed to vanish. I don't recall much about the woman. She didn't say a word."

That night, Connie woke up with projectile vomiting that continued for several days. "I told my Mom and Dad about the 'man' taking me and that I saw the roof of our house from above it. Mom told me it was my imagination. It wasn't. After that, I wouldn't play outside anymore by myself."

The next abduction memory she had was when she was seven and was sitting on her twin bed coloring in a coloring book. "I remember suddenly being tucked under what seemed to be a long thin arm of a weird-shaped entity, a really small entity, and we literally glided up some kind of straight line that looked like a string or beam of light. As we went up, I could hear a high-pitched steady sound."

That was all remembered, but that night she came awake with projectile vomiting. "My sister has vivid memories of the Grays being in our shared bedroom. As adults, we've talked about them."

Her next encounter happened when she was nine. She was playing outside with neighbor kids at her grandparents' house in Atlanta. "We were picking blackberries from a thick patch of vines between the yards. There was a feeling like the ground shifting beneath us and we all looked up. I don't recall what we saw, but the next morning, I woke up and vomited before I could make it to the bathroom."

Those early experiences were just the beginning of a life-long series of encounters with beings that terrorized her and benevolent beings that guided her. Here's another case involving an apparent childhood abduction.

Maurice, a middle-aged engineer residing in Montreal, sent me an e-mail after Trish and I had appeared on *Coast to Coast* with George Noory and talked about *Aliens in the Backyard*. He told me he was a life-long abductee and had never told anyone about it. He said his experiences began in 1975 when he was five years old. His mother had gone into labor so his parents sent him and his older sister to their grandparents' home, where the first incident occurred.

"I know it was late because it was dark. I clearly recall playing in the basement with my tricycle. I looked at the window and saw six gray metallic boots and tight metallic pants covering very skinny legs. Suddenly, a milky white light covered me and I don't remember anything else. To this day, I can't go down into that basement by myself. I shift into a panic mode just at the thought of going down there. This is but one of the numerous unpleasant memories that haunt me."

TRAVIS WALTON

In one of the most famous abduction cases, logger Travis Walton was on his way home to Snowflake, Arizona, riding in a truck with six other men. They had spent the day clearing brush in the Apache-Sitgreaves National Forest and were on a logging road when they supposedly saw a hovering UFO some hundred yards ahead. Intrigued, the men leaned out the right windows for a better look. One of them remarked that it "looked like a crashed plane hanging in a tree."

In *Fire in the Sky*, Walton wrote: "Our growing excitement spurred Mike into wringing out what little speed the pickup could still achieve on the incline. We rolled past the intervening evergreen thicket to where we could have an unobstructed view of the source of the strange radiance. Suddenly we were electrified by the most awesome, incredible sight we had seen in our entire lives.... There, a mere twenty feet above the ground, a strange, golden disc hovered silently."

Walton felt compelled to leap out of the truck and run toward the craft for a closer look. The other men shouted at him to get back in the truck, but he kept moving toward it. When sounds erupted from the craft and it started wobbling on its axis, Walton crouched and a bright, bluish green beam shot from the bottom of the craft. "I saw and heard nothing. All I felt was the numbing force of a blow that felt like a high-voltage electrocution. The intense bolt made a sharp cracking, or popping, sound. The stunning concussion of the foot-wide beam struck me full in the head and chest. My mind sank quickly into unfeeling blackness. I didn't even see what hit me; but from the instant I felt that paralyzing blow, I did not see, hear, or feel anything more."

Walton was missing for five days. Police interrogated his companions, conducted searches of the area where he had disappeared, but he wasn't found. Five days after his disappearance, he called home and spat out his horrifying story: being on a spaceship, surrounded by Grays, escaping in a smaller craft with other humans, finding himself on the highway outside town and seeing a luminous, circular object lift into the dark sky. Walton's experience became a book, then a movie, then another book. Now Walton is in his sixties, and the experience has defined his life.

THE EVIDENCE

It's easy for skeptics to attack anecdotal evidence. Just because you say this happened to you, it doesn't mean it actually did. After all, no abductee has returned from an abduction with photos or video of the insides of a craft or of the beings inside them. Yet, even if they did, the skeptics would probably say it was photo-shopped.

However, some abductees have returned with inexplicable physical scars, rashes, scrapes, marks, nosebleeds, lesions, and sinus problems supposedly caused from implants inserted during the abduction. They have also brought back a contribution to the overall pattern of these experiences, a consistency that turns up time and again during hypnotic regressions.

Not surprisingly, many skeptics are derisive about information obtained under hypnosis. In fact, virulent skepticism led to attacks on John Mack that resulted in a witch hunt in 1994 by the Harvard Medical School. Since Mack was the most academically impressive convert to the idea that abductees are actually experiencing what they professed, the medical school formed a special committee of faculty members to investigate Mack's research. Mack, a tenured professor at the time, hired an attorney, and in August 1995, the committee disbanded without censuring Mack's research.

His contributions to the field before his death in 2004 added to a yet expanding bank of knowledge about the abduction experience. Like Hopkins and Jacobs, he identified a strong sexual/reproductive component to the abductions and to the possibility of a hybrid-breeding program. He acknowledged that the abduction experience doesn't fit into our current worldview. And that was as true in 1999, when *Passport to the Cosmos: Human Transformation and Alien Encounters*, his last book was published, as it is today. "...The alien abduction phenomenon seem(s) to operate so far outside the laws of physics (as traditionally understood) that they may require a new paradigm of reality to include them as real and an expansion of our ways of knowing to explore them..."

HYBRID-BREEDING PROGRAM

Some abductees are shown horrifying scenes of destruction to the planet. The implication is that humanity is responsible for these disasters and that the hybrid-breeding program is a necessary step to ensure the survival of both humans and aliens. So what's involved in this program?

"Hybridization appears to progress in states," wrote David Jacobs in *The Threat*. "It is clear from abduction reports that it starts in vitro with the joining of human sperm, eggs, and alien genetic material. The result of this union, which is "grown" partially in a human female host and partially in a gestation device, is a hybrid being who is a cross between alien and human."

It sounds like a pitch for a movie or a horror novel. When you think about it longer than a minute, the full impact hits you. *If* the evidence gathered over the decades by researchers is true, then we are confronted with even more questions.

How many human abductees have been impregnated and then had the fetus removed? Do the fetuses reach maturity? If so, where are they kept until they do? Is the ultimate goal of this program the take over of the planet? The human race? Are the scenes of global catastrophes that abductees are shown actually going to happen? And what does the government know?

Connie Cannon recalls being taken to an alien nursery where she was shown sickly hybrid children. One of the Grays placed a hybrid child in her arms, indicating that she was its mother. Telepathically, she was told the child would die if she didn't talk to it, and nurture it. "I cried and cried as I held the ugly, deformed little thing."

Diane Fine's story about her unwilling participation in a hybrid program is eerie and baffling. In high school, she was diagnosed with cystic fibrosis disease, had three surgeries by the time she was in her late teens, and was told she would never get pregnant. While living in a college town in upstate New York in 1979, she went to her family doctor because she was feeling so constantly exhausted and frequently nauseated. He conducted a urine test and pelvic exam and informed her she was two months pregnant. He was as shocked as she was.

He deemed her pregnancy to be high risk because of her previous surgeries and referred her to a clinic in Burlington, Vermont to see a specialist. The trip took three hours by car and included a ferry ride across Lake Champlain. On the day of her appointment, Diane set out early with her two roommates. They hoped to explore Burlington before her late afternoon appointment.

"It was a gorgeous spring day," she recalled. "Our drive was going as planned. We passed Dannemora Prison and the town of Dannemora. After this, things got very strange."

Dannemora is part of the town of Saranac Lake and the prison Diane refers to, Clinton Correctional Facility, was a maximum security facility that opened in 1845. From 1900 to 1972, Dannemora also housed a hospital for the criminally insane. Both the town and the prison became synonymous among many New Yorkers for the place where the criminally insane were confined.

Just after passing through Dannemora, Diane and her roommates encountered a dense fog and visibility shrank to zero. If you've ever been caught in dense fog, then you know how eerie it can be—vague shapes around you, that strange dampness in the air, the odor of wetness and earth. It's creepy. They looked for a place to pull over until the fog broke up. They spotted a gravel driveway off to their right, pulled in, and found themselves outside a large old barn that had been converted into a bar/restaurant. They went inside to wait out the fog.

Diane recalls that the couple behind the counter was older, white-haired, short, and friendly. She and her roommates ordered sodas and when she sipped it, she thought the taste was strangely sweet, thick, and warm as it went down. "I had never tasted anything like this before. I have no memory after this point, until two hours later." And that was when Diane and her roommates found themselves at the ferry station, ready to cross the lake to Burlington, with no idea of how they'd gotten there. They couldn't understand how it had gotten to be so late in the afternoon.

They arrived at the clinic just in time for her appointment. She was called into the examining room, where the nurse practitioner read the doctor's referral that Diane was eight weeks pregnant. She examined Diane and immediately seemed confused and called another woman into the room. The second woman also read the referral and examined Diane. The two women conferred for a moment, then the nurse practitioner announced, "This is an unpregnant womb."

Diane was stunned and deeply shaken. "Was the referring physician mistaken?" she asked.

"No, your urine test was positive and he examined you thoroughly. His diagnosis couldn't be wrong. But you are *not* pregnant."

Diane panicked. She suspected that what had happened in the fog, with the missing time, was connected to the fact that she was no longer pregnant. But this was before abductions were a part of pop culture so she didn't have any idea what had happened. Her distress was so acute the clinic gave her a valium, then sent her on her way. When she told her roommates she wasn't pregnant, they were as bewildered as she was.

They headed home along the same route and before reaching Dannemora, looked for the converted barn. "We found the gravel drive, but it didn't lead anywhere. The building wasn't *there*. It was just *gone*, like it had never existed."

She and her roommates never discussed the incident again. It was too weird to talk about and Diane was deeply traumatized. Five years later, she read stories of missing time, missing babies, and aliens. "That's when I knew for sure what had happened in the fog, in that barn bar. My baby was somehow removed from my uterus during that missing time."

An event that mainstream scientists would consider impossible, and even crazy to consider, occurred near a prison whose name was synonymous with insanity. Diane recognized the meaningful coincidence or synchronicity. "It's a dark trickster," she said.

Diane has never recalled any details of what happened during those two hours of missing time. Yet, in 1991, twelve years after that experience, she was abducted and taken to a nursery on an alien craft, where she was shown a sad, sick little baby. "She needed love so badly. It broke my heart. This is when they actually indicated that they had some of my children. Is that a harvest or a kidnapping?"

If it's true that people worldwide are being abducted, floated out through window and walls, and lifted into spacecraft on beams of light, then perhaps the aliens are a type of terrorist that Homeland Security has no way dealing with. No wonder the government's official mantra about aliens and UFOs is that such things don't exist. Since evidence in the usual sense of the word is missing, it's easy to dismiss.

However, if this hybridization program exists, then secrecy may be key to its success. Otherwise, how could vast numbers of people be taken and returned without outside detection? Something is definitely going on behind the scenes of everyday life. But what is it? And what connection, if any, does this all of this have to the dead? That's what we'll examine in the next chapter.

18

ALIENS & THE DEAD

Is there a connection between aliens and the dead? Do aliens move through the spirit world the way we move through our daily world? It's not a subject that many who study the UFO/alien phenomena care to consider. Or, if they do consider it, they might suggest that the dead in such encounters are just more aliens in disguise. In other words, they contend it's just a way of grabbing someone's attention, as if the presence of aliens alone isn't enough.

Likewise, ghost hunters typically don't want aliens mixed up in their investigations of hauntings. Several years ago, the founder of a well established ghost-hunting organization and I were discussing the possibility of co-authoring a book together. When I suggested that we include a chapter exploring the link between aliens and the dead, he was adamant that such a concept didn't belong in the book. "If I wrote a book about ghost hunting that included aliens, I would be the laughing stock of my colleagues."

But of course there are independent thinkers who follow their own passions, their own perspective, even if it results in ridicule. Whitley Streiber, author of numerous books dealing with his encounters, is one of them.

"My own personal observations and experiences, and those of many other direct witnesses, do not suggest that it [close encounters] involves what might be thought of as alien contact, at least not in any way that such a thing might be conventionally understood," Strieber wrote on his *Unknown Country* website in July 2014.

"One of the reasons is the proliferation of encounters that involve not only seeing aliens but also the apparent reappearance of dead people. When having close encounters, people commonly see the dead as well."

Dr. Robert Lanza, M.D., author of *Biocentrism*, suggests that at death we are merely bumped into another universe. So it could it be that beings far more advanced than humans have easy access to that realm, and don't see the dead as dead at all. Take the case again of lifelong abductee Connie Cannon.

DAD & THE ALIENS

After Connie passed her child-bearing years and retired from her nursing career, the number of abductions diminished. Rather than continuing to hide her past, she was willing to tell her story without concern about disguising her identity. She says she doesn't care what people think about her experiences, some of which were included in *Aliens in the Backyard* and *The Synchronicity Highway*, both of which I co-authored with my wife, Trish.

Here's one her stories that relates to aliens and their connection to the dead…or what we perceive as the dead.

"I was in our backyard 12X12 screened gazebo. My mind was drifting in a strange mental state when three black helicopters suddenly appeared overhead. There was no sound of them approaching. They just suddenly were there. I know they were real because my neighbors mentioned seeing them."

Connie said she instantly felt threatened and sick to her stomach. "Just as suddenly, a small disc-shaped craft appeared seemingly out of nowhere and was between me and the black copters. My Dad, or an entity with his identical likeness, was seemingly super-imposed on the outside of that disc and very clearly said, *We've come for Connie.*"

Immediately, the three helicopters vanished, she recalled. "It happened more than once, so I know beyond a shadow of a doubt that my Dad travels in a craft, or seems to travel in a craft. I began to call his craft 'The Cavalry' because when he would come, the bad guys would vanish instantly and I wouldn't be taken."

She added that when it first happened, she thought her dad meant they had come to take her with them, but later she understood that he was saying they had come on her behalf, apparently, to keep the others from abducting her.

Connie remembers seeing the movie *Contact* and sobbing when Ellie, played by Jodie Foster, met her deceased father. She agrees that aliens can take on the image of a loved one, as was the case in *Contact*. But she also thinks that aliens can enter the realm of the dead. "I am convinced, beyond any shadow of any doubt, that when it's time for me to leave, Daddy will come and get me and I'll go home with him......I also believe that we'll leave in a ship through some kind of inter-dimensional portal. If this is all my imagination, then I'll accept it as such, because it brings me a sense of utter comfort to know that when I transition, he'll be with me."

Her father isn't the only loved one that Connie has glimpsed with aliens. She was very close to a retired Army captain who died in 2007. They met when she was thirty-five and 'John' was forty-seven, and their relationship continued until his death.

She had no paranormal contact with him after his death until mid-August of 2014. She refers to the experience as a vivid dream, which took place inside an alien craft after arriving there through an unusual means.

"I glided along some type of almost invisible line that looked like a fishing line or a very thin beam of light. Then I was in a circular room, but oddly, it had a corner in front of me to my left. There were several Grays paying no attention whatsoever to me, and a taller entity in a colorless shimmery jumpsuit, who also paid no attention to me. I felt no fear whatsoever."

Suddenly, an image of John's face appeared in front of her. He looked older than the photos she has of him. "The image vanished and John came around that corner, looking the way he looked when we met in 1977. He was an extraordinarily handsome man with the most astonishingly beautiful shattered-crystal gray-blue eyes. He walked over to me wearing jeans and a plaid flannel shirt. I almost always saw him in uniform or dress clothes in real life, only once in a while in casual jeans, and never in a plaid flannel shirt."

He began talking with her, but she doesn't remember what he said. Then, he unbuttoned the flannel shirt, took it off, and he was wearing a brilliant white shirt. "Whatever he said to me caused me to begin to cry, and I leaned into his shoulder and sobbed."

The experience was more than a dream to her. "I don't know what to call it. I do know there was an encounter with aliens inside a craft and a visitation with a human who is deceased and whom I loved with my whole heart."

Let's assume that Connie's experiences are more than her imagination, that they are actual contact with aliens. Even so, it's difficult to say whether or not the dead who appear with aliens in dreams, or in waking encounters, are spirits of loved ones or aliens in disguise. Is there any other evidence that aliens have an interest in the after-life of humans?

In fact, it seems there is. UFOs have been spotted hovering over cemeteries on a number of occasions.

But why would visitors from elsewhere—if that's who's controlling the UFOs—be interested in cemeteries? If abductions aren't strange enough, the idea of alien crafts camping over graveyards adds an eerie Halloween-ish note reminiscent of ancient legends of monsters skulking among gravestones. When the idea of aliens and the dead come together, many people tend to think of darkness, evil, Satanic rites, vampires, zombies... You get the idea.

It's not what we would expect from the likes of advanced beings arriving at our doorsteps. But perhaps to the aliens, graveyards serve as portals between dimensions, an access point to reach our world.

HIGH-PITCHED SCREECHING

Elk Garden, West Virginia. As of the 2010 census, this community consisted of 232 people. Yet, it has attracted UFOs for more than fifty years, and residents reportedly have seen them in the vicinity of a cemetery adjacent to a Methodist church. The Kalbaughs reside on a farm located a short distance from the Nethken Hill cemetery, and family members say they've seen lights over the cemetery since the late 1960's. They insist that the lights aren't airplanes or helicopters.

Other eyewitnesses agree that the lights were white in color and accompanied by a high-pitched sound, according to Bob Teets, author of *West Virginia UFOs: Close Encounters in the Mountain State* (1994). Maybe sound is a key factor in these reports. Typically, witnesses of low-flying unidentified crafts say the vessels made no sound at all. However, apparently a high-pitched screeching often accompanies sightings near graveyards.

The most memorable and eerie of the sightings over Nethken

Hill took place October 8, 1967, when Reverend Harley DeLeurere and two members of his congregation went up to a promontory from where they had a panoramic view of the cemetery. Intrigued by the stories of sightings, they patiently watched the skies until later that evening when one of the men saw an object described as "a big turtle with lights on it." It appeared over the Nethken Hill and moved deliberately toward the church.

The men were stunned when the luminous turtle-shaped object descended to approximately six feet off the ground and shone its lights at the graveyard. One of the men, referred to by Teets as 'Leonard Jr.,' recalled that the object's lights projected into a day-old grave at the cemetery. "It seems like every time there was a new grave, within the next couple of nights, people would see lights up there."

ORANGE LIGHTS

Another case occurred when two sisters, driving along Route 29 in Chillicothe, Illinois spotted two large orange lights hovering above a cemetery. Simultaneously, the radio station they were listening to abruptly turned to static, according to the report filed with the Mutual UFO Network (MUFON) on June 19, 2011.

The driver immediately pulled into the cemetery and noticed other cars pulling over to the side of the road, supposedly to view the unusual lights. "I watched them for the next few minutes as they just stayed above the cemetery, not moving," the witness said. "The one on the right moved closer to the one on the left, and that's when I saw the top of the larger one."

The object was shaped like a bell or an inverted cone. The base of the object glowed an extremely bright orange and numerous long spikes protruded from the top and curved downward. The witness, whose name was not revealed in the public report, said that after a few minutes the smaller craft moved off toward a field behind the cemetery and the larger one followed.

The two sisters returned to their car and started following the objects. When they reached the high school, they noticed a helicopter heading in the direction the UFOs had taken. "We weren't able to make much sense of it, but definitely believe that the helicopter was following in their direction."

ILLUMINATED CLOUD

In 1977, an unusual event occurred in the town of Gerena, Spain, 14 miles northwest of Seville. On October 23, Ana Rumín and Manuel Fernández were walking along a street near the outskirts of town near where they lived. It was a clear night, the sky studded with stars. Rumín drew her companion's attention to a glow above a nearby cemetery. Fernández assured her that the glow was most likely "a cloud illuminated by the town's streetlights." This seemed a reasonable explanation and they continued down the street.

They saw that the 'cloud' above the cemetery had a reddish hue, and cast its light on the tall cypress trees and the mausoleums. An uncanny silence enveloped the area and they realized that something out of the ordinary was taking place. They stopped at a neighbor's house to get a better look at the phenomenon from his rooftop.

By the time Ruperto Muñoz and his wife accompanied the two witnesses to the rooftop, the red cloud had vanished. But the four onlookers were able to see a small red circular object heading off into the distance. It changed colors from red to green and blinked intermittently before it disappeared in the distance.

Spanish UFO researcher Joaquín Mateos Nogales reported the case and noted that "the area in question offers a wealth of unidentified flying object reports, which we have attested through many years of on-site research."

THE PHOTO

One morning in June 2013, I received an e-mail from Connie Cannon about her son, Kenny, who is also an abductee. Kenny, she wrote, had taken an extraordinary photograph of a UFO outside his home in Maury County, Tennessee, a rural part of the state. He sent her the photo and a description of what he'd seen.

Around 3:50 a.m. on June 23, Kenny was awakened by a "squealing" in his ears and felt "pulled" to go outside. His wife was sound asleep and didn't wake when he got up. As soon as he was outside, the squealing in his ears stopped.

He saw a V-shaped series of glaringly bright, large lights in the night sky. At first, the lights were in front of what Kenny thought was the moon—and the moon on June 23, 2013, was not only full, it was perigee, the closest it gets to the Earth. He rushed back inside the house to grab his cellphone. He was afraid that if he took the time to remove his good camera from the case, the object would be gone by the time he got back outside. He shouted at his wife to wake up, but she didn't move.

When he ran outside again, the brilliant, elongated light that he thought was the moon was still behind the V. He snapped several photos of it. Then, suddenly, the bright light—what he'd mistaken for the moon - 'evaporated.' But the V was still visible, made up of interconnected white lights with a dark shadow surrounding them. It moved slowly toward the northwest. During this time, he turned and saw that the moon was actually in a completely different position in the sky and realized it wasn't the source of the brilliant illumination that had been behind the craft's V-shaped lights.

Kenny snapped photos, trailing the object as it moved. He stopped as he came to a nearby ridge that overlooked an old graveyard and saw a straight red line, like a laser, coming out of the object, and shining on one of the gravestones. Kenny was terrified— not so much by the craft, but by the red beam. It reminded him of the lasers that snipers use on their rifles when pinpointing a target in their sights, and he was afraid it would turn on him. The red beam didn't show up in his photos.

Utter silence surrounded him. He didn't hear any of the typical noises you hear in the south at night—no night birds, no tree frogs, no crickets, no katydids. Just total silence. It spooked him. Even worse, the craft didn't make a sound, either. It took about fifteen minutes before it disappeared behind a distant hill. Kenny desperately wanted to get back to the house, but couldn't move his feet until the V slid completely out of sight.

Badly shaken, he finally returned to the house and fell instantly asleep. As Connie pointed out, "I have a sense he was abducted and that he had just been returned to his bed when he heard the "squealing" inside his head. The squealing prompted him to go outside."

The next morning when Kenny was in the kitchen, his wife rushed out of the bedroom, and threw her arms around him. He asked her what was wrong, and she sobbed that she'd had a nightmare that he was *gone* and when she woke up and saw his side of the bed empty, she thought it was real and that he was *actually gone*. Connie believes that Kenny's wife may have awakened briefly when he was outside—or perhaps in the midst of an abduction— and then had fallen back to sleep.

The next day, Kenny went to the cemetery to locate the grave the object had targeted. Three people are apparently buried there—J.L. Saunders, a man, in the middle; a stepmother, S. Saunders on the left; and a mother, A.E. Saunders, on the right. In the center of the gravestone is a Masonic symbol, the bottom part of which resembles the V-shape of the craft in the photo.

Intrigued by the photos and by the connection to a graveyard, we sent it to Whitley Strieber for his take on it. Strieber had it examined by a photo expert, who said he thought it looked like what one might see when a time-lapse photo of the moon is taken with a hand-held camera. A reasonable conclusion. But Kenny's cell phone is an inexpensive throwaway with a "point and shoot" capacity for photographs—no fancy time lapses, no way to change the exposure, none of the bells and whistles of a digital single lens reflex camera. Connie also explained that when Kenny had first gone outside, he thought he was looking at the glowing full moon. Then the object disappeared and the V-shaped lights became noticeable.

Maury County, Tennessee has known its share of high strangeness. On Dec. 22, 2012, seventeen silent orange orbs floated over the county and were seen by multiple witnesses, and reported on a blog called, *The Vike Factor—Into the Paranormal*. On May 16, 2013, there was an incident that involved a military helicopter and a plane chasing an orb.

Michele Hood of Spring Hill, Tennessee, reported that she and several other adults had seen the chopper tailing the orange orb followed by an illuminated military cargo plane coming from the west. "The helicopter couldn't seem to catch up with the orb. Also, there was a stalled engine sound during the chase—like nothing any of the four adults watching had ever experienced. We get a lot of weird sky activity out here in rural Maury County. Just last night we saw a strange orange orb in the western sky around dusk that stayed stationary, flashed bright."

A case reported by BBC News in 2009 sounded eerily similar to Kenny's experience. The article was headlined... 'UFO fired laser over cemetery,' and included a reference to a high-pitched noise 'like cats wailing.' The sub-heading read: "A UFO was seen hovering over a Cheshire cemetery before firing laser beams, according to a police log released by the government." The case dates back to 1996 and was included in a three-year project to release UFO files by the U.K.'s Ministry of Defense and the National Archives.

Once Connie explained the conditions under which the photos were taken, Strieber invited Connie for an interview on Dreamland to explore the connection between aliens and the dead. Connie was somewhat nervous about going on the radio and requested that Trish and I join her for the interview, which we did. One of the photos Kenny took can be found here: blog.synchrosecrets.com/?p=16439

EXIT 33

Whitley Strieber is a compassionate, yet deft interviewer. He knows his topic and asks the right questions at the right time. He immediately put Connie at ease and she was able to describe her son's sighting in great detail. Strieber was interested in the gravestone that the craft's red laser had pinpointed, specifically the Masonic symbol on the gravestone.

The Masonic symbol was particularly important for Connie. She and her entire family, dating back to the 1700s, are Masonic. Connie is a 33rd degree Mason, as were her father, grandfather and great-grandfather. Because of the way her father died in 1959, Connie's first thought was whether the red light on this particular Masonic gravestone was her father's way of communicating with her.

At the age of forty-two, her father was diagnosed with brain cancer. As he lay in a coma at Emory Hospital, he was unable to speak or see. The cancer had destroyed his speech center and olfactory nerves. Yet, moments before he died, he opened his eyes and pointed at the window and said, "There's a *big ship* over there. I'm going to get on it."

It was medically impossible for him to see, much less speak, and because medical personnel witnessed him speaking, his case caught the attention of medical journals. Connie's contention is that certain groups of aliens are connected to the human afterlife and that her father joined them when he died because at a soul level he was connected with them. "Although my father liked to fish, he always did so from shore. He wasn't interested in boats or boating." So when her father pointed at the window and identified a big ship, she believes he meant a big ship in the sky. She also felt that it was the alien connection that allowed him to speak during the last moments of his life.

The interview with Strieber became a conversation among the four of us that was so deeply strange it was as if we were neighborhood friends sitting around a kitchen table in the middle of the night, discussing the inexplicable, the unimaginable, the unspeakable. But the sideshow that went on before and during the interview was startling.

Before we started, there was an unusual and persistent noise in the studio that Strieber said sounded like a truck. He was baffled because the studio is typically very quiet. Then, during the interview, we were disrupted on a couple of occasions by voices. Strieber would stop and erase the interference, baffled by where it was coming from. When it happened again, he left it in and explained to his listeners what was happening. The equipment was in perfect condition, he said. Everything was in order. Yet, the glitches continued.

At one point, Trish, Connie, and I were talking for several minutes when we noticed that Strieber hadn't said anything. I hurried into Trish's office with a note: Where's Whitley? We quickly realized the connection had failed, so the three of us hung up, and Whitley called us back several minutes later.

As it turned out, he could hear us and apparently continued recording, but we couldn't hear him. Our voices were being recorded, but his wasn't. He said he felt as if he were in "another dimension"—able to hear, but not able to comment.

Isn't this how the dead must feel when they try to connect with us? They can hear us, but can't make themselves heard. They can see us—but we can't see them. They are Patrick Swayze and Demi Moore in *Ghost*. As Strieber put it, "Could it be that we are a larval stage to something greater?"

After re-connecting, we continued without any problems to the end of the interview. Afterward, Strieber wondered if Connie's father had been around and what had caused the EVP - electronic voice phenomena. He had distinctly heard voices on the line that weren't ours, almost as if we were doing the interview over an old-fashioned party line.

The connection between the dead and aliens is like the dark matter in this field, the aspect better left alone, an anomaly among anomalous phenomena. But the question begs to be asked. Does contact with spirits, ghosts and graveyards somehow facilitate alien contact?

THE QUEBEC CONNECTION

When Charles Fontaine heard about the UFO-graveyard story from Tennessee, he felt vindicated. Like Kenny, he lives near a graveyard and experienced something startling there that he relates to UFOs, even though he didn't see a craft. In his case, a dramatic UFO encounter took place in his backyard days after a frightening experience in the graveyard.

Fontaine's story, which is detailed in our book, *Aliens in the Backyard,* involves a possible abduction in the graveyard that resulted in a trip to the emergency room after his pants filled with blood. A subsequent colonoscopy surprisingly detected nothing unusual and the doctor couldn't explain the blood. Days later, at five in the morning, Fontaine and his wife watched mysterious beams of light in the field that separated their property from the graveyard. Then Fontaine spotted a circular craft approaching them in their backyard. That was the last thing they remembered until he found himself taking a shower, and his wife was back in bed sound asleep.

Prior to his encounter, Fontaine had no interest in UFOs or aliens and thought they were fictional creations. Likewise, if there were ghosts or spirits haunting the nearby graveyard, he was unaware of any such activity and skeptical about the possibility. But after his dual experiences and subsequent synchronicities and hauntings, he became convinced that both existed and were somehow related.

That contention, however, didn't sit well with a long-time French-Canadian ufologist to whom Fontaine explained his story. The researcher dismissed the graveyard event, and insisted the story began with the encounter in the backyard.

UFO researcher Scott Corrales noted in an article that, "In an effort to accentuate the positive, we overlook some of these grotesque aspects, mainly because they do not jibe with our concept of an advanced, benevolent, spacefaring, technological civilization—such as one that we may have read about in the books of Larry Niven or Hal Clement. This dark side is raw and primitive, evoking fears that go as far back as the caves, but taking place in our own troubled times. Some of these behaviors suggest—to the discomfiture of many—that the intelligence behind the UFO is far more earthbound than we know, and more closely related to medieval lore than outer space."

WHAT'S IT MEAN?

Researchers have offered a number of possible explanations for why UFOs hover over cemeteries. Even though the reason remains a mystery, possible motives range from the absurd to the grotesque.

One researcher wrote that maybe the aliens had seen long lines of cars with lights on during the day turning into cemeteries so they investigated. Besides the fact that the idea assumes the occupants are mostly clueless about life on this planet, the reasoning also overlooks the point that many cars now have automatic daytime lights.

Another proposed solution suggests that alien implants are in short supply and that the nighttime graveyard visits are all about removing the devices from the recently deceased. A parallel explanation, one that's a bit more practical, proposes that the implants are being deactivated through sound or light. But if the aliens can monitor or track people from a great distance, it seems they could also deactivate the devices from far away as well.

Then there's also an explanation that sounds like a plot element from a B-grade science fiction movie: the aliens are re-activating the bodies of dead humans and turning them into UFO pilots, who are apparently given time to wander about and frighten people. However, given the interest in zombies in recent years, it seems this alternative—the un-living, recycled humans mixing with aliens from who-knows-where—is an intriguing option, at least one with possibilities for the world of horror-based entertainment.

Scott Corrales explored this idea in some depths in his article and provided examples:

A man known only as "Mr. Rible" took his daughter to an airstrip near Butler, Pennsylvania in 1967 to watch for mysterious nocturnal lights known to appear in the area. The father and daughter soon found themselves catching more than a glimpse of the phenomenon when two luminous objects suddenly headed straight for their Volkswagen.

Rather than crashing into the vehicle, the lights abruptly morphed into a half-circle of five humanoid figures "dressed in sloppy green-gray trousers" with their heads covered by flat-topped caps. The exposed skin of their arms and faces was coarse and gave the appearance of being severely burned. Startled by the sight, Rible anxiously turned on the VW's engine and quickly drove around the semicircle of frightening figures.

Corrales wonders if the men-in-black phenomenon, usually related to the early days of the UFO sightings, is connected to the concept of re-animated humans. Stories of encounters with the beings, who typically wear ill-fitting clothes and drive black hearse-like vehicles are well known not only in North America, but also in South America and Europe. Men-in-black outfits usually consist of white shirts, black ties and black suits, common clothing for dead men.

The re-animated human—zombie—concept focuses on the idea that the physical remains of humans are of some value to aliens, that they somehow thrive on dead matter. It's clearly a low-life perspective, far from the concept of star people or benevolent ETs.

THE SPIRIT CONNECTION

The supposed presence of aliens remains an enigma. Anyone who tells you differently is guessing. None of us knows the big picture. While there's plenty of anecdotal evidence to suggest they are here, everything else - who they are, what they are, and what they are doing - is shrouded in mystery. Likewise, their nature—benevolent, neutral, or antagonistic—is unclear. Most likely it's all of the above.

While the Grays seem to be the predominant race, there are stories of other races as well and contact with spiritually enlightened beings. And yet, are the Grays an actual race? According to remote viewer Joe McMoneagle, the Grays may simply be aliens wearing what he calls *skin suits*.

And why should we assume they are from distance planets? They might be time travelers or inter-dimensional beings. If so, then it could be, as I mentioned earlier, that inter-dimensional travelers are using graveyards as portals and might be in contact with the dead, who seem quite alive from their perspective.

Terence McKenna, a lecturer and writer on human consciousness and metaphysics, believed that UFOs are manifestations of the human soul or collective spirit. He thought they exerted psychological influence over the course of history and they would fill our skies and occupy our minds by 2012.

McKenna was off on his dates; a fleet of UFOs has yet to fill the skies. But UFOs do seem to occupy our collective mind. If you search for *UFO videos* on YouTube, nearly six million hits are returned. When you search for UFOs on Google, the hits double.

Researcher Hilary Evans, author of *Gods, Spirits, Cosmic Guardians: Encounters with Non-Human Beings* (1987) and *Visions, Apparitions, Alien Visitors: A Complete Study of the Entity Enigma* (1984) concluded that alien entities may have originated in the minds of the experiencers and are connected with paranormal phenomenon.

In 1957, Carl Jung published *Flying Saucers: A Modern Myth of Things Seen in the Sky* and made a convincing case for UFOs as the unfolding of a modern myth. As Barbara Hannah explained in her biographical memoir, *Jung: His Life and Work*, Jung wasn't interested in whether UFOs were real. The fact that people all over the world were seeing *round objects* in the sky was what intrigued him. "Roundness is the symbol par excellence for the Self, the totality," Hannah wrote. In other words, these round saucers were *symbolic* of an emerging collective need for wholeness.

In the nearly 60 years since Jung wrote his book on UFOs, crafts of numerous shapes and sizes have been reported, physical evidence has been left behind, and thousands of abductees have come forward with their stories. How is that a myth?

But as Dean Radin pointed out in *Supernormal: Science, Yoga, and the Evidence for Extraordinary Psychic Abilities*, "Jung's use of the term 'myth' does not imply that UFO sightings or for that matter encounters with angels, aliens, fairies, spirits, elves or demons are just fantasies. Rather, it suggests that some of these experiences may literally be psycho-physical, a blurring of conventional boundaries between objective and subjective realities." Or, "*mind literally shapes matter, that the imaginal and the real are not as separate as they seem.*"

PREVIEW:

MORE ALIENS IN THE BACKYARD

In the 1950s, the idea of alien visitors meant that beings from other planets somehow traveled great distances in their crafts and arrived here to observe us. If you were a believer, you assumed it would be only a matter of time before these extraterrestrials made themselves known through a public appearance. When that didn't happen, it was assumed that the aliens had realized we were a violent race and contact was too dangerous.

By the 1980s, the believers were becoming divided between those who were convinced that aliens came from other planets—most likely in our own galaxy—and some who suggested the disturbing and mysterious idea that these beings were stranger than we had imagined and were inter-dimensional entities who traveled here from another alternative universe or a parallel world.

Today, nearly half of Americans in polls say they believe that UFOs are alien crafts, and most believers still assume they come from other planets. However, the inter-dimensional perspective has gained considerable traction, especially among hard-core UFO buffs—those who read books on UFO-related matters. To the pro-inter-dimensional crowd, the idea that aliens travel here by spaceships from distant planets is a quaint point of view—sometimes referred to as the 'nuts-and-bolts' perspective. Of course, the inter-dimensional concept is considerably more mysterious than the idea of astronauts visiting from other planets.

That's because during encounters with such beings, paranormal experiences often occur, suggesting that the beings are somehow linked with our brains, our consciousness. The beings communicate telepathically and seem as if they are literally inside of us as well as outside of us. They appear and disappear, move effortlessly through walls, levitate, and travel in crafts that maneuver abruptly at speeds that would kill humans.

The best way to explore the concept of such beings is through the stories of encounters, through anecdotes. Numerous so-called abductees have described terrifying experiences, especially their encounters with the Grays, slender four-foot-tall beings with oversized heads and large black eyes that seem to wrap around their faces. But there are other beings reported as well, and some people report positive experiences. Sandy Simmons, not her real name, is one of them.

Sandy is a retired veterinarian, whose story is astonishing because of the frequency of contact and its peculiar nature. Clearly, she is not dealing with entities that exist in physical reality in the same sense that we do. She describes her visitors in terms of quantum physics. "The beings I work with exist primarily in a wave state and we, as humans, exist as particles. They've been teaching me to exist partially in a wave state and they have learned to exist partially in a particle state."

In other words, our world is more dense than theirs, but apparently they are able to manipulate the subatomic world so they can appear here to some extent. The way she describes the nature of the beings is essentially the definition of light, which acts both like a particle and a wave. So the entities could be called 'beings of light' or inter-dimensional beings.

Even though they can communicate telepathically, they don't hold conversations with Sandy. Instead, they work with energy. She has kept journals about her experiences since they began in the mid-1990s.

One of her regular visitors is a being that stands more than seven-feet-tall and has long, thin arms and legs. His head is small and oval, with a concave forehead and no obvious mouth or nostrils. His eyes are round and protruding, like those of an insect. His torso, in contrast to his lengthy, gangly limbs, is short and triangular and he has no defined shoulders or hips.

She refers to him as 'John' because his real name is unpronounceable. In spite of his startling appearance, Sandy allows him and other alien visitors to perform their 'energy work.' Here's a description from Sandy's journal of the first energy session with the being that she would come to know as John. She seems comforted by the presence of a guide she refers to as Gabriel, who she felt would protect her.

AUG. 7, 1996

Thursday I was told they (the ETs) will be working more with my physical body to prepare me to meet them. Although I think I'm ready, my brain wouldn't handle the things I will see and feel. I thought this physical contact would be at a subtle level. Then Saturday night (Aug 3rd), I went to bed around midnight and as I was lying on my back my feet suddenly started to sway side-to-side! (Not so subtle!) I clearly experienced someone (something) lifting and moving my feet and legs!

I was wide awake, yet couldn't see anything. But I clearly felt the presence of Gabriel, so I stayed with it. Then, it progressed to a palpation of my torso, deep but gentle. At one point, the swaying and rocking of my feet and legs became very exaggerated, as if the entire bed was swaying. Then, I suddenly shut down and slept. (Jay came home about 3 a.m., after this had happened).

Last night (Aug 6) was incredible! As I lay on my back, pressure was applied to my feet. Then I was turned onto my right side and the pressure was applied to my legs. It was firm, but comfortable. I then realized I was being turned over onto my belly, and as I lay there, relaxed, the mattress started to roll under me like waves.

I was alert, not even tired. I held my breath to see if that was contributing to the unmistakable, very real, sensation, but the mattress continued to move. The bed then 'tipped upwards.' Even though it felt like it was actually moving, visibly the bed remained still. This is difficult to comprehend, let alone describe. It rocked and swayed, I was upside-down and sideways. That was the actual sensation. It was really amazing.

I saw a tall single being who was moving the mattress in this way. He was shadowy and had a familiar male energy. Slender and strong. When I first set eyes on him I sat up in shock and cried out "This changes everything!" In my head I heard a simple "Yes." I was shaking in disbelief and said, "We are so much more than we think we know." And again I was told, "Yes."

CONFIRMATION

If Sandy's story were hers alone, it would be easy to dismiss her experiences as vivid dreams or an overly active imagination. However, Sandy's experiences have been shared by her husband and her ex-husband, both of whom have had related encounters. In fact, her ex-husband, who is also a veterinarian, even wrote the charter for a proposed organization called The Center for Inter-dimensional Studies that intended to document and explore these encounters.

Her husband, George, works for the county government and only has a moderate interest in UFO-related matters. He never researches or reads books on the subject. However, he's supportive of Sandy's explorations and has glimpsed the beings himself. He has also experienced some of the physical phenomena associated with their visits. In particular, he has felt the bed moving in a dramatic wave-like motion beneath him, a phenomenon that Sandy calls the 'high seas,' and he has seen orbs and other images that appear in the house.

The beings touch Sandy as part of their energy work, but avoid direct contact with her skin. "The touching they do with me is a powerful, energetic interaction," she wrote in an e-mail. "When I talk about the body and bed waves, it is nothing subtle and almost impossible to describe to someone who hasn't experienced it. The high seas or body waves started within the second or third session with the being I call 'John' and continue to this day. My work with the beings has allowed me to deal with an enormous amount of energy without being 'burned' on a cellular level."

SANDY'S EARLY LIFE

Encounters with interdimensional beings, as Sandy refers to them, have been a regular part of her life for two decades. But her mysterious experiences go back to her childhood.

The first incident occurred when Sandy was about nine years old, home by herself and playing in the living room. Her experience was so strange that she didn't dare tell anyone. She was on the sofa, pretending it was a ship at sea and the room was the body of water. The ship was sinking, so she had to swim to an 'island' across the room—a chair in the corner about ten feet away.

She made a swimming motion towards the chair, and in that instant she floated from the sofa over to the chair. "When I reached the chair, I clung to it, wide-eyed, my heart racing. I felt that I had just done something very wrong and I could never, ever tell anyone about it. I ran from the room and hid, trying to grasp what had just taken place."

Sandy's fear about telling anyone about her experience was probably related to growing up in a dysfunctional family. Her father was a navy officer and bacteriologist and worked as the commanding officer of a bacterial warfare research program. She describes him as violent and controlling, often pointing guns at family members whom he ruled with physical abuse and intimidation. He was a veteran of two wars and Sandy thinks he might've suffered from post-traumatic stress disorder (PTSD).

Her mother, Gina, was an unhappy woman, who yelled and argued and threw things. After years of fighting, her parents divorced in 1970, and the mother and five children moved to a smaller house in Braddock Heights, Maryland. Sandy's three older sisters soon moved away, leaving her and brother to deal with their mother's erratic behavior.

Gina was a difficult and bitter woman, who ranted and screamed, blaming everyone for her divorce and lack of money. She became friends with a middle-aged Latin American woman in the new neighborhood, who was involved in black magic. Even though Gina had been a devout Catholic, she was anxious to learn all she could about the dark arts.

She soon met a man at a bar, a low-life alcoholic, who moved into their house. Sandy found him disgusting and wanted nothing to do with him. And for good reason. When Gina was out, he repeatedly tried to molest her. She fought him off every time, but didn't get any help from her mother. When she told Gina about it, she said it was Sandy's own fault and that she deserved it.

A mainstream psychologist might consider Sandy's experience of floating across the living room as a literal flight of fantasy, an escape from her difficult home life. But Sandy says that when she was growing up, she focused on all the good times, especially when she spent summers on her grandparents' farm. She remains convinced that the floating event really happened, and served as a hint for what would come. As she grew older, her life would increasingly include experiences outside of the realm of the daily world.

At age 17, Sandy fled home and never returned. Even though she hadn't graduated from high school, had no money, no car or driver's license, she ended up living and working on a beautiful sheep farm that had a small commercial laboratory. She finished high school in 1976, and for the next five years became the manager of the farm/lab operation. If anything, the disturbing events of her childhood had served to move her out into the *real* world at an early age, not into a world of escapist fantasies.

SIGHTINGS

During those years at the farm, more unusual events occurred. She saw her first full-blown apparition when a man dressed as a Civil War officer came through a closed bathroom door, walked past her, and went right through another door in an old, historic house. The ghost was harmless, but it scared the hell out of her. She also experienced visions, particularly of faces and places she didn't know, and she saw auras around some people.

Once, she was with a lover and he freaked out because they were surrounded with a blue and yellow light that looked like the 'snow' one would see on a TV station that signed off for the night. She just accepted these events without much thought because she was too busy with the farm responsibilities to let it interfere with or influence her life.

She also had numerous nebulous experiences with short beings, three to four feet tall, that watched her from the doorways of the various barns on the property. At the time, she thought they were some kind of ghost-children because of their size. She had no other explanation for their presence. "I used to see them clearly out of the corner of my eye and would whip around sometimes and whisper 'gotcha,' hoping to catch one off guard before it vanished. Now I think they were most likely the 'visitors' hanging around."

UFO ENCOUNTER

Even though Sandy is in frequent contact with other-worldly beings, she doesn't consider herself an abductee and, in fact, has encountered a UFO on just one occasion. It took place in 1977 and had a strong impact on her, not something she could easily dismiss.

It was evening in early October and she was sitting at a table, reading a Leon Uris novel. Her right arm was broken and in a cast as the result of a fall from a horse the week before. The front door was open and her dog, Daibando, popped the latch on the screen door with his nose and let himself out, as he always did when he needed to relieve himself

Ten minutes passed and she started wondering what could be taking him so long. Daibando rarely left her side, so when he went outside, he always came back within a few minutes. Finally, puzzled by his absence, she stepped outside, gazed toward the barns and called his name.

She was about to call again when she felt something was wrong. Her skin started to tingle and crawl. She whipped around and saw a massive, incomprehensible thing moving slowly over the mountain. It was a huge, triangular-shaped vessel of some sort, gliding in absolute silence. It was slightly domed underneath and rounded in the back with small silvery white lights along the rim. On the underside were four larger white lights and several green lights.

Sandy froze like a deer in the headlights and just stood there dumbfounded as this giant craft glided overhead and headed south. It was there and gone in a matter of seconds. Yet it all seemed to happen in slow motion, and shudders of fear whipped through her entire body. Suddenly, her dog trotted down from the barn area, his ears flattened back against his head as though he was confused or distressed. She quickly put him in the house, closed the door, and ran in a panic up to the main house.

Cathy, the farm owner, answered the door and Sandy blurted out what she had just seen. She was shaking and stammering as Cathy led her into the kitchen and gave her a glass of wine to calm her down. She described the craft in detail, asked if there was anyone she should call. Cathy thought of the local military base, because they might know if there were any test crafts in the area.

Sandy talked to a man at the satellite tracking station who said there were no test flights taking place. He became very interested in her story and told her that he knew of a state police sergeant and another officer who recently witnessed a UFO in the area. Sandy called the local state police station and the sergeant was on duty. He was helpful and told her whom to call to report the sighting.

She contacted someone with a 202 area code, which includes Washington, D.C., and told her story. The next morning, three young men showed up at the farm and began asking her questions. They had a tripod and camera, tape recorders and compasses and explained how this area was a hotbed of UFO activity.

They handed her an inch-high stack of reports about UFOs and mentioned that the neighbor across the street, a wealthy businessman, recently reported a similar sighting. Other reports were from residents of Burkittsville, less than a mile away, who recently had awakened in the middle of the night when smoke alarms were set off. When they went outside, a powerful humming vibration was heard throughout the town.

One of the men took Sandy aside and asked if she would be willing to go to the Camp David area on Saturday. She agreed to go, but when her mother heard about it, she said, "Don't do it Sandy, he's one of them."

Sandy burst out laughing because that was a ridiculous thought, especially coming from her mother, who then repeated the warning. By the time she ended the call, Sandy was so confused and frightened that she immediately called the man and told him she couldn't go. He was upset and wanted to know why, but she cut the conversation short and hung up. It was all getting too weird for her. She just wanted to get back to her normal life.

MOVING ON

In 1981, Sandy moved to Durham, N.C. to attend college, with plans for a career in science. Six years later, she was accepted into veterinary school, and it was there that she met the man she would marry, and with whom she would share many of her strange experiences with the so-called inter-dimensional beings.

One day, she was out at the vet school barn, training one of the young horses, and a man came up to the paddock fence to watch. They greeted each other and he introduced himself as Jay. He was in the junior class, two years ahead of her. After that, they would see each other in the halls of the clinic or in the library, and wave.

It was synchronicity—meaningful coincidence—that would bring them closer together. Sandy needed to move closer to vet school and find a cheap apartment, because the one-hour commute every day was brutal. But apartments were scarce. She had only two days before she had to move, and still hadn't found a place she could afford.

Stressed out, with newspaper in hand, she was on the way out of class to look at more apartments when she ran into Jay. They chatted and she told him her predicament. To her surprise, he excitedly said his roommate just quit school and moved out that week and he was desperate for a new housemate! He lived a mile away from school, Sandy's share of the rent would be $125 a month, and dogs were allowed. She still had her German Shepherd, Daibando, and couldn't believe her luck. She moved in on Valentine's Day, 1988, a potent symbol of the relationship that would develop.

Jay graduated the following year and they got married. But the first two years turned into a long-distance relationship when Jay moved two hours away to practice at a clinic in coastal North Carolina. Meanwhile, Sandy remained in Raleigh to finish her degree.

The day after she graduated in May of 1991, she drove to North Carolina to join Jay, but on the way something strange happened. She had made the journey on Route 70 many times and was familiar with the road. She was cruising along at 65 mph through the darkness on the empty road when a huge ball of light appeared out of nowhere and started to follow her just a foot or two from her rear bumper.

At first, she thought it was a crazy motorcycle rider, but the ball of light was too big and too bright to be a headlight. She was about a mile from Jay's exit and was watching the ball of light when a voice in her head told her to take note of the time. She glanced at her watch. It was exactly 10 p.m.

She started to exit the highway and the ball of light disappeared. When she arrived at Jay's place a few minutes later, she was still shaking and dazed by the experience. She opened the car door, but couldn't move. Jay came out to greet her and she told him about what had happened. They went inside and thirty minutes later her brother called to tell her that their grandmother had just died—at 10 p.m.

"She was the one person in my entire family whom I adored and admired and she was so proud that the first doctor in the family was a woman!"

Shortly after her graduation, Sandy and Jay moved to Annapolis, Maryland where she was hired by a vet clinic. At first, everything went well and she adapted to her new routine. Then, one day a few months into her job, she woke up and was horrified to see seven quarter-sized dark blotches on the left side of her neck. They looked like huge, dark hickies that had just appeared overnight.

"As soon as I saw these horrible marks in the mirror, I knew they were somehow related to the extraterrestrial-type beings from years ago. I woke up Jay and showed him the marks, then told him about the ET and UFO experiences I had in my past. He was completely confused by the whole situation.

"I went to a dermatologist, hoping that there was some medical explanation for these marks, but he had no explanation for acute onset of such a large area of hyperpigmentation. He tried to treat it anyway, with no results."

The disfiguring marks remained for several years and she knew deep down that they were indicators of some sort, a constant reminder that there was something she needed to address internally. Meanwhile, things started to get difficult at the clinic. She discovered that her boss was beating animals. Disgusted, Sandy turned in her resignation, but her boss convinced her to stay, assuring her it would never happen again.

But it did, and she stayed on, uncertain what to do about it. Eventually, she would make a difficult decision, but she did so only after the beings reappeared in her life.

WATCHER

In 1995, a tall white entity that she called Watcher started to hang around, standing at the edge of the yard and looking towards the house. She called him Watcher because that was what he did, nothing else. Then one night, a small female being about three-feet tall appeared at her bedside. Sandy was fully awake as the being stood about a foot away from her face. The being's body was a glowing cobalt blue, as if she were holographic rather than a physical being.

"I had a deep love for her, and I greeted her as if it was natural for me to see her there. She let me know that she was always with me and we communicated effortlessly via non-verbal thought. I thanked her for visiting me and told her she was very beautiful.

Her eyes were deep and wise and the only way I can describe our relationship is that she is a part of me."

Sandy called her Blue.

Soon afterwards, she decided to speak out against her boss and his animal abuse. Doing so was a difficult challenge. She was a relatively new vet, and he was well-liked and well-established in the community. She was also frightened by the man's capacity for violence. She consulted with a lawyer who was horrified and insisted she turn the case over to the states attorney's office right away, rather than try to deal with it on her own.

"I wanted to handle it as quietly as possible because I didn't want it to get out to the media and I wanted to protect the technicians who were my witnesses. It was an ugly situation and I started to panic and cry when I suddenly experienced a 'God-zap,' a sweep of powerful energy that passed through me. It's like a laser beam lightning bolt that comes in through the top of your head and explodes inside of your cells and your very soul with an incomprehensible purity that is Love unlike anything we think of as love on this earth. There is no thought during this experience, just overwhelming passion, joy, love, peace and awe."

Ultimately, she reported her boss to a veterinarian administrative organization and he received psychiatric help. She left the clinic a short time later and the four-year-old marks on her neck finally started to fade. They disappeared completely by the summer of 1996.

By then, the beings were visiting her regularly, performing their energy work. Here's a journal entry from that time.

AUG. 22, 1996

I got home about 6:45 pm and sat on the bed quietly with my eyes closed to calm down. My crown chakra was humming intensely. There was a powerful energy coming in, but I received no visions or eye flutters. Eventually I lay down and John appeared instantly. Right away he started the typical work on my feet and during the process it occurred to me that all the pulling and pushing and waves were some sort of magnetic field that he uses to "move" me. It reminds me of the feeling you get when holding two magnets of the same polarity against each other. It creates a resistance so that the magnets repel each other energetically.

He moved up to my legs and I decided to try something. All this time he has worked on me I have noticed that he only touches the parts of my body that are covered by the sheet. So I put the sheet over my head this time to see what would happen, and he went straight to my face! (It was the first time he touched my head at all). He worked a lot on my forehead (6th chakra area) and even touched my lips.

At one point I laughed out loud because he came down my forehead with his finger and playfully "beeped" my nose! The realization that I was working with a being that seemed to understand humor was profound! This suggests a possible emotional intelligence, or at least one that understands the human emotions. For me, this is a giant leap in getting to know this fellow.

After a while I got up and did a little work on the computer. I went to bed about 9 p.m. and John appeared again. I could see him very clearly and I noticed that he would slow down and even stop his work on my legs when I opened my eyes. At one point when I was looking at him he started to wave his arms back and forth like windshield wipers. At the time I thought it was part of the work he was doing, so I didn't think much of it.

I closed my eyes again and he continued to work. When I opened my eyes, he would stop and step back. Over and over. Soon the message was very clear to me. He doesn't want me to touch him or look at him, and he won't touch my bare flesh. The arm waves were a signal for, "No, don't do that."

John and I have a difficult time with verbal communication. He uses hand signals and gives me visuals when he wants to communicate, or he talks to Jay, who can understand him. I feel that it may have something to do with frightening me, which he doesn't want to do.

A few times, I panicked when he was working on me because he was so physically close to me. Keeping my eyes closed allows me to remain centered and focused. So, I again covered my head with the sheet and right away he went to work on my forehead, touching and rubbing, causing strong pulses in that area. He was even willing to touch my hands for the first time, as long as they were under the sheet.

I had my eyes open the entire time I had the sheet over my head and I could clearly see his shadow moving around above me through the sheet. Again, this suggests true density! After about forty-five minutes, I was very tired and told him enough, said goodnight and went to sleep.

Probably the most remarkable aspect of Sandy's descriptions of the activities of the being she calls John is that, for the most part, she seems so calm and accepting of his presence and his manipulations of her body. All of it is done without verbal communication. Keep in mind that the creature hovering over her is definitely a 'bump-in-the-night,' being, one whose mere appearance—described earlier—would terrify most people.

Another remarkable comment in the journal entry was the mention that Jay was also in contact with the tall, lanky being. More on that coming up.

SPIRIT GUIDES

What makes Sandy's story even more interesting and somewhat unique is that in addition to the frequent visits by these non-human inter-dimensional beings, she also mingles with the spirit world. In early 1995, she met her three guides. She became aware of their presence. She began to meditate and met Riba, Jean-Paul and Adam. "Riba always stood behind my left shoulder. She wore Egyptian garb and had the traditional Egyptian hairstyle, but her face was not entirely human. Her features were very feminine, but smaller and set lower on her face than typical human features, and her skin was milky white."

During one meditation, she was in an out-of-body state with Jean-Paul and experienced a precognitive event. He was driving an old pickup truck and she was riding in the seat next to him. They were moving slowly over a bumpy country road when suddenly a small red and white plane fell out of the sky and crashed in a field near the side of the road.

She watched the plane flipped over right before impact and she could see two people hanging upside-down in the cockpit with their seat belts still on. She shouted that they had to help them, because the plane was going to catch fire. But when Jean-Paul just kept driving along very slowly, Sandy got angry and started to pound on the dashboard, screaming that he had to stop.

"I could see the male passenger was moving a little, groping at his shoulder, but the woman pilot was just hanging there and she looked severely injured," she wrote in her journal. "Blood was streaming down from her head and through her blond hair. I was hysterical, but Jean-Paul calmly drove on, saying that the plane wouldn't catch fire, and they would be all right."

A couple of days later, Sandy heard a brief statement on the radio news that a small plane had crashed in the next county. It caught her attention, but she blew it off as coincidence. The next day, she opened the local section of the newspaper, and there was a story describing the plane crash she had witnessed in detail, exactly what she had seen with Jean-Paul. The article said the pilot and passenger had survived, even though the red and white plane flipped over. The woman was in critical condition and the man in guarded condition in the hospital. They were found hanging upside-down in their seats and fortunately the plane hadn't caught fire.

"I think Jean-Paul demonstrated to me that I need to control my emotions, especially when it involves seeing something that leaves me feeling helpless. If I'm going to see future events in the work we're doing, I can't get so emotional about the situations I might observe."

JAY'S CONNECTION

Jay was aware that Sandy was having metaphysical experiences, but he just shrugged it off, and continued to focus on building his career. He was eccentric in many ways, a difficult person to live with, a man with serious anger issues. During college, friends had warned Sandy not to get involved with him. As a married couple, they often went their own ways, pursuing their own careers.

Then, in late 1995, Jay began having his own visions. He would close his eyes to relax and the visions would come to him. One consistent vision was a man dressed in battle fatigues standing in front of him. When Jay finally greeted him, the man introduced himself as Davy. He told Jay that they'd been close friends in the past, and that Davy died in a war.

Then Jay started to receive visions of a very odd being he called the "Blue Meanie." This entity never did anything mean to Jay, but would be in his face every time he closed his eyes, silently looking at him. He was all blue with a shadowy, somber human face, and he wore a strange, jester-type hat. Jay kept pushing him away mentally until one day in a vision he came charging toward Jay, waving his arms.

This freaked Jay out and Sandy told him to confront this being and demand an explanation the next time it happened. So he did and the being softly said, Take my hand. He then led Jay on an astral travel to a huge white sphere of light that Jay called a "giant snowball," because it was cold to the touch. Once inside the sphere, the Blue Meanie suddenly transformed into a bright white angel, who towered almost ten feet tall over Jay and had the face of one of his favorite high school teachers. He then introduced himself as Archangel Gabriel.

'Gabriel' told Jay the reason he used the strange appearance before was to get his attention, that if had he appeared as an angel Jay would have ignored him completely because he didn't believe in angels. He called Jay a 'Warrior of the Light,' and said that he had been a warrior in many past lives. Later, he also explained that Jay tended to be coldly objective, because it served him to be that way as a warrior in the past. But now it was time to heal. Gabriel also said that Jay's general loathing toward other people was also past-life related in that he felt people would never change, never learn.

On many occasions after that day, Jay was shown his past lives through his angelic guide. Most were simple lives, but there was also a lot of war and violence in his past. Gabriel had a wonderfully gentle sense of humor, and for the first few months, Jay was belligerent about having an angel in his life, because he thought it might disrupt his career. At one point, Gabriel stood before him, smiling softly, shaking his head and stroking his beard. "Jay," Gabrielle said, "what am I going to do with you?"

Sandy laughed when she heard the story and told Jay that he was the only person she knew who could frustrate an archangel. Over the next year Jay went through an astonishing transformation, becoming much more warm and loving. Even his family members noticed and asked her what had happened to him.

Here's one of Sandy's journal entries that includes an experience that she shared with Jay. It begins with a description of her unusual type of contact with seemingly benevolent alien beings.

SEPT 20, 1996

Last night they did something new; they took my feet and pressed both soles together, lining up the balls and toes of each foot, and held them firmly in place. I had surges of that static-like energy rush through me and then there was a bright white flash in my face. This didn't occur in my head like a vision, but had an exterior source, like a camera flash going off right in front of my closed eyes, only much brighter. I then had a clear vision of an old man struggling to stand, then I saw the legs and feet of something not at all human just stomp right through my visual field.

When we woke up this morning, two ETs were standing at the foot of the bed. Jay and I sat up in amazement and looked at them. He muttered, "Do you see that, do you see that?"

I laughed and said, "Yeah, pretty incredible, isn't it."

They faded, as if they just wanted us to see them and nothing more. Jay then told me about his recent conversations with these two beings. He said they claimed to be Sirian and one said to call him Marshal. What a funny name for an ET. I thought they would have weird names like Zolar or something. They informed him that I had a Pleiadian, with some Sirian background, and that he was 100 percent Sirian. Jay and I both feel this information is bizarre, but I'll record it and make no judgment one way or the other.

Throughout 1995 and into1996 Sandy and Jay established a new bond. A purpose had come into their lives and Sandy was not so angry anymore at Jay's egocentric behavior. They felt connected in the work they were doing with the beings that had come into their lives. In general, Sandy was dealing with the ETs, such as John, Watcher and Blue, and Jay was in a different program with more focus on angels and healing his anger and insensitivity. "Our paths were the same as our marriage; together yet separate," she recalled.

Surprise, Surprise!

Then George came into her life.

In May of 1996, she was chatting with a friend on AOL, and was about to sign off when she received an instant message (IM) from a stranger. That happened a lot and she was about to blow him off. But she hesitated. He said her screen name caught his eye and he felt a need to IM her. Her screen name was Sister7, based on the Pleiades. He didn't know the meaning of the name, but just liked it.

At first, she thought he would be a typical jerk trying to pick her up online. But instead she found him polite and sincere. He told her he was married with two daughters, and recovering from surgery related to a perforated ulcer that almost killed him. They became friends on line, and always kept their conversation light.

A couple of weeks later, she told George about her ET involvement, and that she'd just had contact the day before with a being she called Watcher. George wrote back: "Sandy, I know about those guys. I know what you're talking about!" He then proceeded to explain the UFO experience he had with a friend at age fourteen. Their online conversations were more heart-to-heart after that day.

During one such conversation, she was looking at the screen, waiting for his next sentence to come up, when she gasped and sat upright in her chair. She sensed he was right there, standing behind her, and she felt an incredible surge of love. Excited, she typed, "You were just here!" At the exact same time, he wrote: "I don't know what just happened, I just spaced out for a minute."

They acknowledged their deep love for each other after this experience and it threw her into a panic. It was confusing and didn't make sense. She thought the beings were testing her and she became angry. After all, she was a faithful wife in spite of her difficult marriage. She was fighting the feelings in her heart for George, who she'd never met in person, and trying to convince herself that she was being ridiculous. They were both married and had different lifestyles. She'd never even seen a photo of him, but somehow she knew what he looked like, and even what he wore every day.

A couple of months into her online relationship, Sandy heard something from Jay that stunned her. Jay's guide Gabriel told him, "Tell Sandy to let you go. You are one of Sandy's blocks." Even though she was being drawn to Florida, she was resisting for fear of hurting Jay. Gabriel's declaration just made her angry.

"I was furious. It seemed that after eight years, I finally had a reason to stay with Jay, with all the work we were doing with the angels and ETs, and now I was being pulled away," she wrote to a friend a couple of years later. "I'll never forget that day in my living room when I shook my fist in the air and yelled at the top of my lungs, 'Butt out, Gabriel, I am not your pawn!'"

Finally, she made up her mind to tell Jay about George. She was going to ask Jay to help her fight off her feelings for the man. "I came into the room where Jay was reading and sat down, very depressed and stressed out. Just before I opened my mouth, Gabriel came in with such force it threw me back into the chair. My eyes rolled back and fluttered uncontrollably and the top of my head felt as if it was coming off. I told Jay that Gabriel was here and wanted to talk to him."

Jay put down his book, closed his eyes for a few minutes, then opened them and said, "Wow, that was weird." Gabriel had warned Jay of dangers ahead. Sandy understood and didn't mention George. She decided she would handle the situation on her own.

She decided to fly to Florida and meet with George, essentially to say hello and goodbye. She was convinced that once they were face-to-face, she would fully accept that they were from different worlds and end her silly fantasy. It had been twelve years since she'd had a vacation, and she'd been telling Jay all year that she wanted to go on a mini vacation somewhere on her own. She decided that she could accomplish two things by going to Florida. She'd always wanted to see the Gulf coast, so she booked a waterfront room in Clearwater for four days.

George knew her intentions were to meet, then part as friends and return to her life with Jay, and he supported her decision. The problem was that George would never have been able to get away from home, even for an afternoon, because his wife kept close taps on his whereabouts. But an astonishing and unlikely synchronicity unfolded that allowed George to spend the weekend with Sandy. George's wife decided to take a cruise on those same days and she took their daughters along, leaving George alone. So he drove up to Clearwater where Sandy was staying.

When Sandy first saw him, she realized he was a very sick man, still close to death even though it had been four months since his surgery. He was emaciated and pale, a mere one hundred and twenty-five pounds. His eyes were sunken and dark and he was an emotional wreck. In their on-line talks, he had never said anything bad about his wife of twenty-two years, and avoided talking about her. That weekend Sandy learned that she was extremely abusive, constantly screaming at him. He was a quiet and humble man and only stayed with her to protect his daughters, since she spread the abuse to them as well.

He cried in Sandy's arms with an agony that made her cry too, and she performed a healing on him that had a powerful affect. They then spent the next two days enjoying each other's company, telling stories and laughing, as if they were old friends.

She fell even deeper in love with George, but Sandy was still determined to return to her marriage. George didn't want to interfere, so when she left, it was with the understanding they would never see each other again. "It was a painful goodbye, but I used every ounce of will I had to return to my regular life."

George, on the other hand, decided to leave his wife. His youngest daughter had turned eighteen, and he knew that if he didn't end the marriage, he would die.

For the next few weeks, Sandy couldn't stop thinking of George and was miserable. Finally, she realized she wasn't listening to her heart and knew she needed to be with him. She sent him an email and explained her feelings. He was suffering too and prayed silently she would return to him. He was overjoyed with her decision. She visited him again a couple of months later and that was when he started to experience the 'God-zaps' and they started to simultaneously share visions.

She told Jay she wanted to move to Florida someday, but she had no idea it would happen as fast as it did. He suspected there was a man involved, but didn't want to discuss it. The beings had told him that Sandy needed to let him go. He also knew that she had a difficult time in cold weather and would be happier in the warmer climate. Sandy finally understood Gabriel's efforts to get Jay involved in her decision to leave. "I experienced that marvelous moment of clarity, that instant when the heel of the palm makes sharp contact with the forehead and the words, 'Oh, I get it,' fall from the lips."

Jay was understanding and willing to let her go—thanks to the intervention of the beings. But Sandy had no idea that when she returned from her trip a drama was about to unfold in which her dealings with the beings would be turned into something scandalous.

Upon her arrival home from Florida, she had only $50 to her name and would be losing her lab job when the grant money ran out at the end of the month. Money was tight, but nevertheless she used the $50 to buy her mother a birthday present. She found an exquisitely illustrated book on angels and drove up to see her that weekend, excited about giving it to her.

Over the past couple of years, her mother seemed to have taken an interest in spiritual growth, and Sandy did everything she could to encourage it so her mother would avoid her destructive tendencies. She even planted a perennial flower garden in her yard and called it her healing garden with the hope her mother would gain gentleness through the beauty of nature. She also told her mother about the beings and how she accepted their presence and appreciated their energy work.

While she was kind to her mother, Sandy also would stand up to her meddling and manipulations, and abusive behavior towards her or her siblings. But on the day before her mother's birthday, everything was fine between them. Later in the day, one of Sandy's sisters called and announced that everyone was chipping in to buy mom a big TV for her birthday and she wanted $150. Sandy explained that she didn't have any money and that she already gave mom her birthday present. Her sister seemed to be okay with that and said nothing more about it.

However, a few days later she received a call from her mother, who started screaming about Sandy not helping pay for the television. Then, when Sandy tried to respond, she slammed down the phone. At first, Sandy was crushed because she'd given her a very special present from her heart. Then she became angry because her entire family was upset with her.

After Sandy stopped taking their calls, her mother turned on her completely and told everyone in the family that Sandy was possessed by demons. She took everything Sandy had shared with her about the beings and twisted it into a horrible pack of lies. She started calling Sandy's friends, old classmates and coworkers and telling them Sandy was a member of a cult.

Sandy couldn't believe it. All of this over a stupid TV? She was totally dumbfounded. She had never been mean or cruel to her family. It just wasn't part of her nature. But now she knew it was time to turn away. Meanwhile, her plans to move to Florida were already evolving. With Jay's support, she prepared to quietly depart in April of 1997. Jay, following Gabriel's urging to protect Sandy, fended off inquiring family members and helped her to get ready to leave.

In spite of her efforts to avoid her family, an incident occurred that—except for the help of one of her guides—would have exposed her plans to quietly disappear. As she was shopping for some Florida clothes at the mall, she suddenly received an urgent message from an angelic guide. She was told to go visit Joan, a long-time friend she hadn't seen for months. It was an odd request, since she had no plans to see Joan before she left. In fact, Sandy didn't like being around her very much because Joan tended to be nosey and pushy.

However, she was aware that Joan knew she was moving. She'd found out through a friend of Jay's. Sandy immediately left the mall and drove to Joan's house, dropping in unannounced. Joan was surprised to see her and made a pot of coffee. They sat down at the kitchen table and were exchanging casual comments when the phone rang. It was Sandy's mother. She yelled at Joan so loudly that Sandy could hear her. Joan just hung up and said to Sandy, "I was just attacked, on my phone, in my home, by your mother!"

Sandy's mother had no idea she was there at the time. However, Sandy was certain that if she hadn't been there, Joan would have revealed her plans. Her mother called a minute later and left a threatening message on Joan's answering machine. It gave Sandy goose bumps as her mother spoke in a voice that reverberating with rage. "You dare hang up on me Joan, you dare to do that? Just you wait, you'll pay, you'll be sorry, just you wait...."

Joan gave the answering machine the finger and said, "Screw you, Gina."

Sandy left town the next day and Jay waited a month before he told her family that she'd left. Sandy gave him a post office box address and a voice mail number that couldn't be traced to an address. She sent letters to her brother and sisters that were gentle, but firm. She wanted nothing to do with them and their bad behavior, and to please respect her privacy. But that didn't stop them.

Her brother called the police in Sarasota with an outrageous story that she was a victim of domestic violence. He also called Jay and threatened to put up missing person's posters all over Sarasota and even flew to Florida where he staked out her mailbox for three days.

Sandy finally threatened the family with restraining orders and a lawsuit charging character assassination. They still tried to harass her and Sandy's mother even called some of George's clients seeking information about her. But they couldn't find out where she lived.

Her family continued to make Jay's life difficult with repeated calls and threats, but he fended them off. Two months after Sandy's move, Jay lost his job and found a new one in California, so he was also able to escape.

Sandy married George in September 18, 1998, a year and a half after moving to Florida, and following her divorce from Jay. A wedding photo shows the couple on the beach at Siesta Key, near Sarasota, with a rainbow streaking down from the heavens to Sandy's head. "It rained all day and stopped twenty minutes before the ceremony," she recalls. She and George have lived in Sarasota ever since, and Sandy continues to experience regular contact with the beings.

ABOUT THE AUTHOR

Rob MacGregor resides in South Florida. He writes fiction and non-fiction. He has won the Mystery Writers of America Edgar Allan Poe Award. His most recent non-fiction books, written with his wife Trish MacGregor, are *The 7 Secrets of Synchronicity*, *Synchronicity and the Other Side*, and *Aliens in the Backyard*. He also co-authored *The Everything Dream Book* and *The Lotus & the Stars: The Way of Astro-Yoga*.